WEBER

HOT & SPICY

BEST RECIPES FOR YOUR BRAAI

JAMIE PURVIANCE

First published as *Weber's On The Grill: Hot and Spicy*
in the USA in 2014 by Weber-Stephen Products Co.

This South African edition published in 2016 by Struik Lifestyle
an imprint of Penguin Random House South Africa (Pty) Ltd
Company Reg. No. 1953/000441/07
The Estuaries, 4 Oxbow Crescent, Century Avenue, Century City 7441
PO Box 1144, Cape Town, 8000, South Africa
www.penguinrandomhouse.co.za

ISBN 978-1-43230-518-5

For Weber-Stephen Products LLC
Author Jamie Purviance
Editorial, design and production rabble + rouser, inc.
Chief Creative Director Christina Schroeder
Creative Director Shum Prats
Art Director Carrie Tilmann
Photographer and Photo Art Director Tim Turner
Photo Assistants David Rainy, Joe Bankmann
Editorial Director Marsha Capen
Editor and Writer Abby Wilson
Digital Guru Christy Clow
Food Stylist Lynn Gagné
Assistant Food Stylist Nina Albazi

Contributors Lynda Balslev, Brigit Binns, Lena Birnbaum,
David Bonom, Elizabeth Hughes, David Joachim, Rick Rogers,
Cheryl Sternman Rule, Andy Schloss, Terri Pischoff Wuerthner

Colour imaging and in-house prepress Weber Creative Services

Round Mountain Media
Susan Maruyama, Consulting Global Publishing Director

Weber-Stephen Products LLC Mike Kempster, Board Member;
Brooke Jones, V. P. Global Marketing

For Penguin Random House South Africa (Pty) Ltd
Managing director Steve Connolly
Publisher Linda de Villiers
Managing editor Cecilia Barfield
Design manager Beverley Dodd
Typesetter Randall Watson
Editor and indexer Gill Gordon
Proofreader Anita van Zyl

Printing and binding Toppan Leefung Packaging and Printing
(Dongguan) Co., Ltd, China
Reproduction Hirt & Carter Cape (Pty) Ltd

Weber-Stephen Products LLC is represented in South Africa by
Weber South Africa, 141 Hertz Close, Meadowdale, 1614, Johannesburg.
www.weber.co.za
www.weber.com
www.penguinrandomhouse.co.za

Table of Contents

Thirst. It may be the single biggest reason that so many of us crave hot and spicy foods. We thirst for adventure, we thirst for excitement, and we thirst for flavours that jolt our senses and make us feel alive. Of course, after eating fiery foods, we also experience a more literal thirst – a thirst we tend to quench with large glasses of cold, frosty drinks. Perhaps that's why braaiing spicy foods goes hand-in-hand with parties and entertaining.

Happily, there are countless ingredients that allow us to create flavourful and nuanced heat. From fresh chillies to dried, from sauces to peppercorns, from ground roots to spicy seeds, the braaiing enthusiast's pantry of zesty seasonings is vast and deep. Want smoke with your heat? We can do that. Want a condiment with a kick to slather on meats, vegetables and fish? It's in these pages. Want a red-hot rub to transform your entrée from good to unforgettable? We're on it.

Your job here is simple: to prep your palate for bold flavours and to invite your friends and family along for the ride. Hot and spicy braaiing is made for unfussy gatherings and is perfect for casual, impromptu celebrations. Even better, many of the marinades and sauces in these pages can be prepped ahead of time, freeing you up later to braai without stress and to enjoy the company of your friends and family.

If you're worried about the intensity of the heat in this book, don't be. These recipes were designed to create big flavours, not to scorch your tongue or make your eyes water. Plus, each recipe is clearly rated on a heat scale from 1 to 10 (with 1 being very mild and 10 being super spicy), so you can see at a glance how intense the results will be. There's a huge middle ground represented, too – foods that are perfect for the moderate heat lover, for the one who appreciates the thrill of a piquant sauce, a vibrant rub, or a snappy spice blend but who still wants to be able to taste the interplay of other flavours. In other words, we've made sure to include something in here for everyone. Proteins range from beef to lamb, from pork to poultry, and across the seafood universe. We've got a generous chapter for vegetarians, too, and a slew of sauces, seasonings and sides.

As always, we'll prep you in the pages that follow with everything you need to know before you step outside to light the braai. In fact, the rundown of hot and spicy ingredients at your disposal is likely to surprise you. (You may not have realized just how many unique ways there are to punch up the heat of your favourite foods.) We'll also offer expert advice on how to handle the more unusual ingredients. Above all, though, our goal here at Weber is simple: to arm you with the basics, to guarantee superb results, and to let you experience the freedom and joy of braaiing spicy foods in your own way.

Go ahead and grab yourself a drink. It's about to get hot around here!

Jamie Purviance

Braaiing Fundamentals

KNOW YOUR CHILLIES

To the uninitiated, chillies are a mysterious breed. Their heat and flavour hide behind brightly coloured exteriors, and if you're not familiar with the differences in one chilli to the next, you've got some serious surprises in store. See, the heat in chillies can vary wildly, both between different varieties and even within a single variety from one individual chilli pepper to another.

Chillies are often ranked by where they fall on the Scoville scale, a rating system for that burning-on-the-tongue sensation named for chemist Wilber Scoville in the early twentieth century. The number of Scoville heat units (SHU) corresponds directly to the amount of a fiery compound called capsaicin concentrated in a chilli's seeds and membranes, and the scale ranges from zero to more than 1,000,000. Pure capsaicin measures in at between 15 million and 16 million SHU. Sweating yet?

The next few pages are a primer on the fresh, dried and powdered (ground) chillies you'll encounter in the recipes that follow. They are listed according to their SHU, from mildest to hottest.

FRESH CHILLIES

BELL PEPPER Bell peppers are your garden variety sweet chilli peppers with the bell-like shape. While they don't pack any heat, and thus merit a zero on the Scoville scale, bell peppers do add a crisp juiciness, vivid colour (green, red, yellow, orange or even purple), and a sweet or slightly bitter flavour to braaied dishes. Peppers can be braaied whole without any oil, then briefly covered so their skins can steam, loosen and be easily peeled. Whenever possible, choose large, flat-sided peppers for braaiing, to maximize the surface area that comes into contact with the cooking grates.

0 SHU

JALAPEÑO Originating from Jalapa, Mexico, these dark-green, triangular chillies are about five centimetres long and sport blunt, rounded tips. Their considerable heat can be tempered, if desired, by cutting out their seedpod and veins with a paring knife (*see* page 10) either before or after braaiing. Jalapeños are popular not only braaied but also raw, pickled, stuffed or dried and smoked, in which case they are known more commonly as chipotle chilli peppers (*see* page 8).

2,500–9,000 SHU

THAI Though it is petite, don't let the Thai chilli's cute size fool you: this chilli packs a considerable wallop in the heat department completely disproportionate to its dimensions. Green or red (the redder the colour, the riper the chilli), these two-centimetre-long, narrow, thin-skinned Southeast Asian peppers prove beyond a doubt that small chillies can be very, very powerful.

50,000–100,000 SHU

HABANERO Vivid orange when fully ripe, these small, lantern-shaped chilli peppers are prized not only for their not-so-subtle heat, but also for what some consider to be a fruity flavour. At only about four centimetres long, habaneros top the heat index for the fresh chillies commercially available in supermarkets.

150,000–325,000 SHU

BELL PEPPERS

JALAPEÑO
CHILLIES

THAI CHILLIES

HABANERO
CHILLIES

DRIED CHILLIES

As chillies ripen, they change from green to red, yellow or purple. When dried, their colours darken, their flavours change and they get hotter, because the seeds, which hold most of the capsaicin, make up a larger proportion of dried chillies. To cook with dried chillies, you need to soak them to soften their leathery skins.

ANCHO Called poblano in their fresh form, the wide, flat ancho chilli pepper has a fruit-forward, raisin-y sweetness and an occasionally bitter edge that's still relatively mild and aromatic.

1,000–2,000 SHU

CHIPOTLE These dark-skinned, dried and smoked jalapeños are popular the world over for their deep, smoky flavour, a flavour heightened by the velvety, vinegary adobo sauce in which they're often canned.

5,000–8,000 SHU

ANCHO CHILLIES

DRIED RED CHILLIES

CHIPOTLE CHILLIES

GROUND CHILLIES

PAPRIKA Spanning the spectrum from sweet and mild to sharp and hot, paprika – the result of grinding red chillies multiple times – is often associated with Hungary, where it features prominently throughout that country's cuisine. Most paprika is pretty mild, but it complements the other chilli powders and adds its own great colour.

SMOKED PAPRIKA This intensely smoky form of paprika (called *pimentón* in Spain, where it is prized) is produced by smoking red chillies over oak fires. It can be mild and sweet, or piquant and hot. This is often the undisclosed ingredient in braai masters' special spice rubs.

PREPARED CHILLI POWDER Chilli powder is an amalgam of chillies, herbs and other aromatics, such as garlic, cumin, coriander and clove. When cayenne and crushed red chilli flakes are added (alone or in combination), the chilli powder is marketed as hot, but otherwise, expect it to be fairly mild.

ANCHO CHILLI POWDER When ancho chillies alone are pulverized, this deep reddish-brown powder provides a moderate level of heat with notes of dried fruits and coffee.

CHIPOTLE CHILLI POWDER Intriguing only begins to describe the complexity of this smoky powder that somehow manages to blend sweet, fruity flavours with fairly hot spiciness.

CRUSHED RED CHILLI FLAKES Crushed red chilli flakes – the disk-like form of a combination of any of the heat-forward chillies – add texture, flavour and fire when used to finish a dish.

GROUND CAYENNE PEPPER Long, slim, and bright red when fresh, cayenne chilli peppers are most often used in their dried, powdered form. Named after the Cayenne River in French Guyana, cayenne is a popular seasoning that, with just a slight dusting, can really kick up the heat in marinades and seasonings.

Braaiing Fundamentals

PREPPING CHILLIES LIKE A PRO

STEMMING AND SEEDING JALAPEÑOS

Using a paring knife, cut off and discard the stem ends. Cut each chilli in half lengthways, then slip the knife tip under the central seedpod and remove in a single, fluid stroke. Slip the knife under the long veins to remove as well. (Only remove the seeds and veins if you specifically want to mitigate the heat.)

MAKING YOUR OWN HOT SAUCE

Chilli fans rave and debate about their favourite store-bought hot sauces, but if your interest in sauces borders on an obsession, you will make your own, partly because you can dial the firepower up or down by using as many or as few chillies as you like. Roast the chillies first with some garlic on the braai, then purée them in a blender with rum, lime juice and salt. See page 136 for the full recipe. Remember to use gloves when handling hot chillies, and don't lean right over the blender. The fumes could burn your eyes or lungs.

HANDLING
CHILLIES Some people choose to wear kitchen-grade, disposable latex gloves when handling chillies. This ensures that any residual oils or capsaicin on your hands will be discarded with the gloves before you inadvertently touch your eyes or other sensitive areas of your body. (The oils can remain on your skin even after a careful hand wash; this is especially important to remember when handling super-hot chillies, like habaneros.)

BRAAIING WHOLE CHILLIES

Peppers and larger or smaller chillies can be roasted whole and dry over direct heat, turning with tongs until well charred all over. Transfer them to a paper bag (or place in a bowl covered tightly with cling wrap) and leave to steam for about 10 minutes to loosen the skin. Slide the skin off with a knife or your fingers.

TOASTING AND SOFTENING CHILLIES

Dried chillies can lend a lot of flavour to a sauce or marinade if you prep them properly. The first step is to cut them open and shake out the seeds. Then toast the chillies in a hot cast-iron pan for about 30 seconds per side. Finally, soak the pods in hot water until soft and pliable, about 30 minutes. Now you can drain, destem and purée them easily with other ingredients.

Braaiing Fundamentals

THE ESSENTIAL HOT AND SPICY PANTRY

In addition to fresh chillies, dried chillies and ground chillies, get creative and stock up on these other heat-forward ingredients. Alone, but especially in combination, they'll add an extra layer of intensity to your braaied dishes.

ROOTS

Don't forget about oft-neglected roots like wasabi powder, prepared horseradish and fresh ginger – taste bud ticklers that can bring muted flavours to energetic life. Though they start their lives underground, once they hit the palate, they move front and centre, demanding attention in dishes like Ginger Curry Lamb Chops with Yoghurt Sauce (page 44), Marinated Lamb Racks with Rhubarb-Horseradish Chutney (page 46), Turkey Escalopes with Wasabi Brown Butter and Mizuna (page 78) and more.

PEPPERCORNS

Ground black, white and green peppercorns wake up the palate with their bold, sharp and distinctive bite. Recipes that take advantage of these dried berries include Porterhouse Steaks with Brandy Black Pepper Butter (page 26), Pepper Skirt Steak with Daikon-Orange Relish (page 35) and more.

GROUND MUSTARD SEED

Mustard seed, mustard powder and prepared spicy or Dijon mustard all deliver a swift flavour boost and golden-brown colour to marinades, sauces and glazes. Mustard features prominently in the Pork Burgers spiked with Peppers and Mango Mustard (page 52), Mustard-glazed Chicken Wings (page 64), Beer Can Chicken glazed with Molasses and Hot Mustard (page 72), Smoked Tandoori Salmon with Tarragon-Mustard Sauce (page 94) and more.

SAUCES

Chilli-based sauces like Tabasco, mild chilli sauce, Chinese-style chilli-garlic paste, Sriracha and Thai curry paste are a busy cook's ready-made flavour grenade. A few spoonfuls straight from the tube, bottle or jar infuse meat and vegetable preparations with complex notes of heat and spice that are already seasoned and balanced. The best part? They're shelf-stable and, once opened, last for months in the fridge. Examples of their good uses include Thai-marinated Chicken with Spicy Dipping Sauce (glaze contains Sriracha) (page 67), Lemongrass Prawns in Lettuce Leaves (contains Thai red curry paste) (page 83) and more.

BRINGING THE HEAT AND FLAVOURS TOGETHER

Keep in mind that when braaiing, or using any other cooking technique, your end goal doesn't really waver from recipe to recipe: you want to create balanced, full-flavoured dishes whose ingredients harmonize and complement one another seamlessly. This holds true if the flavours are big, bold, hot and spicy – as they are in these recipes – or even if they're subtle or more delicate, like those you may encounter in other cookbooks. The key concept is balance. A full-on heat blast will shock your palate and prevent you from appreciating the interplay of tastes, including salty, sweet, sour, bitter and umami. Add the inimitable smoky flavour you get when braaiing, the caramelized flavours you achieve through the

Maillard reaction, and the cleansing flavours of whatever you're drinking (for you will be quaffing something refreshing when consuming all this spicy food!), and there's a real smorgasbord of opportunity here for creating magic.

To achieve that magic, take advantage of the numerous ingredients that allow you to find that all-important balance. You've got acidic ingredients, like citrus juices, tomato, yoghurt and vinegar; sweet elements, like white or brown sugar, maple or golden syrup, honey, agave nectar and molasses; and salty elements, like anchovies, olives and capers, to name but a few.

As you play around with these recipes and make them your own, you'll start to braai with confidence. A well-stocked pantry, an abundance of chillies and their derivatives, and an appreciation of how to balance flavours will all serve you well when you step outside, light up your braai, and feast on the hot and spicy dishes that follow.

Braaiing Fundamentals

BRAAIING KNOW-HOW

THE DIFFERENCE BETWEEN DIRECT AND INDIRECT COOKING

With direct heat, the fire is right below the food. With indirect heat, the fire is off to one side of the braai, or on both sides of the braai and the food sits over the unlit part.

Direct heat works great for small, tender pieces of food that cook quickly, such as steaks, hamburgers, chops, deboned chicken pieces, fish fillets, shellfish and sliced vegetables. It sears the surfaces of these foods, developing flavours, textures, and delicious caramelization. If you place foods thinner than 3 cm over direct heat they'll be cooked all the way to the centre in just minutes.

Indirect heat is generally better for larger, tougher foods that require longer cooking times, such as whole chickens and pork shoulders.

An area of indirect heat is also helpful as a 'safety zone', which is a place where you can move food temporarily if it begins to flare up over direct heat. If you set up a part of the braai with low indirect heat, you can keep food warm there until you are ready to serve it.

SETTING UP YOUR CHARCOAL BRAAI FOR DIRECT AND INDIRECT COOKING

First things first. You'll need fuel, and the simplest way to measure the right amount of fuel for your charcoal braai is to use a chimney starter. Use it like a measuring cup for charcoal. Fill it to the rim with briquettes or lump charcoal, and burn them until they are lightly covered with ash.

Spread the coals in a tightly packed, single layer across one-half to two-thirds of the charcoal grate. Put the cooking grate in place, close the lid, and let the coals burn down to the desired heat. Leave all the vents open. This basic configuration is called a two-zone fire because you have one zone of direct heat and one zone of indirect heat.

preheat the braai for 10–15 minutes. Then simply leave all the burners on and adjust them for the heat level you want.

With gas, you can switch from direct to indirect heat almost immediately. Just turn off one or more of the burners and place the food over an unlit burner. If your braai has just two burners, turn off the one toward the back of the braai. If your braai has more than two burners, turn off the one(s) in the middle of the braai. The burners that are left on can be set to high, medium or low heat, as desired. Whenever the food is over an unlit burner and the lid is closed, you're braaiing over indirect heat.

It's the setup you'll use most often. The temperature of a two-zone fire can be high, medium or low, depending on how much charcoal is burning and how long it has been burning. Remember that charcoal loses heat over time.

SETTING UP YOUR GAS BRAAI FOR DIRECT AND INDIRECT COOKING

There's nothing complicated about lighting a gas braai. However, gas braai operation does vary, so be sure to consult the owner's manual that came with your braai. To light a Weber® gas braai, first open the lid so unlit gas fumes don't collect in the cooking box. Next, slowly open

the valve on your gas cylinder all the way and wait for one or two minutes for the gas to travel through the gas line. Then turn on the burners, setting them all to high. Close the lid and

Braaiing Fundamentals

ESSENTIAL BRAAI TOOLS

TONGS

Definitely the hardest working tool of all. You'll need three pairs of tongs: one for raw food, one for cooked food and one for arranging charcoal.

BRUSHES

Choose a solid, long-handled brush with stainless steel bristles. Use it to clean off the cooking grates before you braai and during braaiing.

PERFORATED GRILL PAN

Here's a great tool for cooking small foods that might otherwise fall through the cooking grate, like mushrooms and cherry tomatoes. Remember to preheat the pan before the food goes on.

CHIMNEY STARTER

This is the simplest tool for starting lump charcoal or briquettes faster and more evenly than you could with firelighters. Look for one with a capacity of at least 5 litres.

INSTANT-READ MEAT THERMOMETER

Braaiing without a thermometer is like running in the dark. It leads to unforeseen troubles. Get yourself a reliable instant-read thermometer that can tell you how far along your food is at any moment.

BAKING TRAY

A baking tray (sheet pan) is a handy, portable work surface for oiling or seasoning foods, and there's nothing better to use as a landing pad for hot food coming off the braai.

BASTING BRUSH

A good brush is always helpful for oiling raw food evenly before it hits the braai, as well as for applying sauces and glazes. Brushes with stainless steel handles and silicone bristles can go into the dishwasher.

BRAAI GLOVES

Use these to protect your hands and forearms when managing a charcoal fire or when reaching towards the back of a hot braai.

SPATULA

A long-handled spatula with a bent (offset) neck (where the blade is set lower than the handle) is great for sliding under delicate foods and turning them without breakage.

TIMER

Say goodbye to burnt steaks and dry pork chops that were left on the braai just a minute too long. A timer never forgets when you should make your next move. Get one that is loud enough for you to hear, no matter how far you wander.

18

BEEF

20 Bacon Cheeseburger Sliders with Spicy Tomato Sauce
22 Moroccan Kofta Kebabs with Red Pepper Couscous
24 Too-Good-To-Be-True Sloppy Joes
25 Caribbean Beef Kebabs
26 Porterhouse Steaks with Brandy Black Pepper Butter
28 Smoky Red Hot T-bone Steaks with Tomato-Chilli Salsa
29 Charred Chilli Beef Kebabs with Guacamole
30 Mustard Prime Rib with Horseradish Cream
32 Thai-marinated Flank Steak with Sambal Olek
34 Spicy Beef Satay with Coconut-Peanut Dipping Sauce
35 Pepper Skirt Steak with Daikon-Orange Relish
36 Thai Beef Salad with Cashews

LAMB

38 Butterflied Leg of Lamb with Aromatic Spice Rub and
    Dried Cherry Chutney
40 Lamb Kebabs with Zhoug Dipping Sauce
42 Chilli-rubbed Lamb Kebabs with Spicy Tomato Sauce
43 Spicy Lamb Meatball Pitas with Yoghurt Sauce
44 Ginger Curry Lamb Chops with Yoghurt Sauce
46 Marinated Lamb Racks with Rhubarb-Horseradish Chutney

PORK

48 Coriander Pork Burgers with Spicy Slaw
50 Spicy Pork Meatball Sliders
52 Pork Burgers Spiked with Peppers and Mango Mustard
53 Savoury Pork Souvlaki with Greek Salad
54 Beer-simmered Brats with Spicy Onion Relish
56 Pork Fillets with Green Chilli Sauce
57 Pork and Mango Skewers with Vietnamese Dipping Sauce
58 Pork Vindaloo with Raita
60 Pork Yakitori with Braaied Sweet Potatoes
61 Crispy Shredded Pork in Lettuce Cups with Chillies and Lime
62 Slow-cooked Pork Carnitas

POULTRY

64 Mustard-glazed Chicken Wings
66 Chicken Breasts with Chipotle-Tequila Glaze and Melon Salsa
67 Thai-marinated Chicken with Spicy Dipping Sauce
68 Spicy Jambalaya

70 Tangerine Chicken
71 Basque Chicken Halves with Peppers, Smoked Ham
    and Olives
72 Beer Can Chicken Glazed with Molasses and Hot Mustard
74 Chicken Fra Diavolo
75 Chicken Chilaquiles
76 Spiced Duck Breasts with Chipotle Cherry Salsa
77 Chipotle Turkey Burgers with Pickled Onions
78 Turkey Escalopes with Wasabi Brown Butter and Mizuna

SEAFOOD

80 Prawn tails with Bloody Mary Cocktail Sauce
82 Spicy Prawn Tostadas with Roasted Vegetable Salsa
83 Lemongrass Prawns in Lettuce Leaves
84 Braaied Scallops with Chilli Dipping Sauce
86 Smoked Black Mussels in Spicy Marinara over Linguine
87 Griddled Linefish Escabèche with Citrus and Chillies
88 Spiced Yellowtail with Mango-Avocado Salsa
90 Yellowtail with Jerk Seasoning and Papaya Salad
91 Cuban-spiced Tuna Tacos
92 Hake and Sweet Potatoes with Mustard-Lemon Aïoli
94 Smoked Tandoori Salmon with Tarragon-Mustard Sauce
95 Braaied Salmon with Smoky Tomato-Chipotle Sauce
96 Braaied Potato Salad with Smoked Trout, Red Onion,
    and Spicy Greens

VEGETARIAN

98   Sweet and Spicy Nuts
99   Smoky Brinjal 'Caviar'
100 Vegetable Muffuletta
102 Beetroot and Apple Salad with Horseradish Dressing
103 Potato Flapjacks with Horseradish Applesauce and
     Watercress Salad
104 Braaied Corn Chowder with Roasted Tomatoes
     and Chillies
106 Stuffed Red Peppers with Jalapeño Pesto
108 Summer Vegetable Pasta with Spicy Ricotta
109 Courgette Fritters with Herbed Lemon Crème Fraîche
110 Black Bean Burgers with Chipotle Sour Cream
112 Falafel Patties with Tahini-Garlic Sauce
113 Korean BBQ Tofu with Sesame Spinach

BACON CHEESEBURGER SLIDERS
WITH SPICY TOMATO SAUCE

PREP TIME: 20 minutes
BRAAIING TIME: 6 to 8 minutes
LEVEL OF SPICINESS: 4/10

4 slices bacon
500 grams red onions, each halved lengthways
    and thinly sliced
1 teaspoon finely chopped fresh thyme leaves
1 teaspoon sugar
¼ teaspoon coarse sea salt
¼ teaspoon ground black pepper
½ cup tomato sauce or ketchup
1 tablespoon hot chilli-garlic sauce, such as Sriracha

Patties

1 kg lean beef mince
2 tablespoons Dijon mustard
1½ teaspoons coarse sea salt
1 teaspoon Worcestershire sauce
¾ teaspoon ground black pepper

6 thin slices mature cheddar cheese, cut into quarters
12 small dinner rolls or cocktail rolls, split
2 plum tomatoes, each cut across into 6 thin slices

1. In a large pan over medium heat, fry the bacon until crisp, 10–12 minutes, turning occasionally. Place the bacon on paper towels to drain. Add the onions, thyme and sugar to the pan and cook until the onions are tender and lightly golden, 10–12 minutes, stirring occasionally. Season with the salt and pepper.

2. Prepare the braai for direct cooking over medium-high heat 200°–260°C (400°–500°F).

3. In a bowl, whisk the tomato sauce and Sriracha.

4. Gently combine the patty ingredients. With wet hands, form 12 loosely packed patties of equal size, each about 1.5 cm thick. Don't compact the meat too much or the patties will be tough. With your thumb or the back of a spoon, make a shallow indentation in the centre of each patty. This will help them cook evenly and prevent them from puffing on the braai.

5. Brush the cooking grates clean. Braai the patties over ***direct medium-high heat***, with the lid closed as much as possible, until cooked to medium doneness, 6–8 minutes, turning once when the patties release easily from the grate without sticking (if flare-ups occur, move temporarily over indirect heat). During the last minute of braaiing time, place two quarter slices of cheese on each patty to melt and toast the rolls, cut side down, over direct heat.

6. Spread some spicy tomato sauce on each bottom bun half, and top with a patty, a tomato slice, bacon and caramelized onions. Serve right away.

SERVES: 6

20

MOROCCAN KOFTA KEBABS
WITH RED PEPPER COUSCOUS

PREP TIME: 30 minutes
BRAAIING TIME: 8 to 10 minutes
SPECIAL EQUIPMENT: 4 long flat metal skewers
LEVEL OF SPICINESS: 2/10

Kofta

700–800 grams lean beef mince *or* lamb mince
1 medium onion, coarsely grated
⅓ cup finely chopped fresh Italian parsley
    or coriander leaves
2 Thai chilli peppers, seeded and finely chopped
1 tablespoon crushed garlic
1 tablespoon paprika
2 teaspoons ground cumin
1½ teaspoons coarse sea salt
1 teaspoon ground ginger
1 teaspoon ground coriander
½ teaspoon ground cinnamon

Couscous

1 tablespoon extra-virgin olive oil
1 medium red pepper, cut into 1.5 cm dice
2 cups water
¾ teaspoon coarse sea salt
1 cup quick-cooking couscous

Extra-virgin olive oil
2 tablespoons finely chopped fresh coriander
    or Italian parsley leaves
1 lemon, cut into wedges

1. In a large bowl, combine the *kofta* ingredients, blending well with a fork. (You can finely chop the onion, chillies, garlic and herbs in a food processor instead, and stir in the remaining ingredients with a fork.) With wet hands, form 12 oblong patties of equal size, each about 10 cm long. Thread three *kofta* lengthways onto each skewer, pressing firmly to adhere to the skewers. Refrigerate the kebabs until ready to braai.

2. Prepare the braai for direct cooking over medium-high heat 200°–260°C (400°–500°F).

3. In a saucepan over medium-high heat, warm the oil. Add the red pepper and cook until softened, about 3 minutes, stirring occasionally. Add the water and salt and bring to a boil over high heat. Stir in the couscous. Remove from the heat, cover tightly and let stand until the couscous is tender, about 5 minutes. Fluff the couscous with a fork, cover the saucepan again and set aside to keep warm.

4. Brush the cooking grates clean. Generously brush the *kofta* all over with oil. Braai the kebabs over **direct medium-high heat**, with the lid closed as much as possible, until the *kofta* are nicely charred on the outside and the centres are still slightly pink, 8–10 minutes, turning once or twice. Remove from the braai.

5. Divide the couscous evenly among four plates. Slide three *kofta* onto each portion of couscous and scatter the coriander on top. Serve warm with the lemon wedges.

SERVES: 4

TIP!

To call *kofta* 'meatballs' is a bit of misnomer, as they are oblong and are threaded lengthways onto flat skewers for braaing. Metal skewers work best for *kofta*, as bamboo skewers may be too thin and flimsy to support them.

TOO-GOOD-TO-BE-TRUE SLOPPY JOES

PREP TIME: 15 minutes, plus about
45 minutes for the sauce
BRAAIING TIME: 1¼ to 1¾ hours
SPECIAL EQUIPMENT: instant-read thermometer
LEVEL OF SPICINESS: 4/10

Rub
1 tablespoon paprika
1 tablespoon packed brown sugar
2 teaspoons garlic flakes
2 teaspoons coarsely ground black pepper
2 teaspoons coarse sea salt
1 teaspoon chilli powder

1.5 kg deboned beef chuck
Extra-virgin olive oil

Sauce
2 tablespoons extra-virgin olive oil
1 cup finely diced red onion
1 cup finely diced red pepper
2 teaspoons crushed garlic
1 tablespoon all-purpose flour
1 tablespoon prepared chilli powder
1¾ cups beef stock
1 can (410 g) diced tomatoes in juice
½ cup barbecue sauce

Coarse sea salt
Ground black pepper
8–10 hamburger buns, split

1. Combine the rub ingredients. Lightly brush the meat all over with oil and season evenly with the rub. Leave to stand at room temperature for 15–30 minutes before braaiing.

2. Prepare the braai for direct and indirect cooking over medium heat 180°–230°C (350°–450°F).

3. Brush the cooking grates clean. Sear the meat over *direct medium heat*, with the lid closed, about 15 minutes, turning occasionally. Slide over *indirect medium heat* and continue braaiing, with the lid closed, until an instant-read thermometer inserted into the thickest part of the meat registers 70°C, 1–1½ hours more. Remove from the braai and leave to rest while you make the sauce.

4. In a large saucepan over medium-high heat, warm the oil. Add the onion and red pepper and cook until the onion is soft and lightly browned, 8–10 minutes, stirring occasionally. Stir in the garlic and cook for 1 minute more. Add the flour and chilli powder, stirring to combine. Add the stock and bring to a boil over high heat, whisking occasionally. Stir in the tomatoes and the barbecue sauce. Lower the heat and simmer until the mixture is the consistency of gravy, about 30 minutes, stirring occasionally. Cut the meat into bite-sized pieces, add to the sauce and simmer for 10–15 minutes. Season with salt and pepper. If the sauce is too thick, thin with ¼ cup water.

5. Brush the cooking grates clean. Toast the buns, cut side down, over *direct medium heat*, for about 30 seconds. Spoon the meat onto the buns and serve immediately.

SERVES: 8 to 10

24

CARIBBEAN BEEF KEBABS

PREP TIME: 30 minutes
MARINATING TIME: 4 to 6 hours
BRAAIING TIME: 6 to 8 minutes
SPECIAL EQUIPMENT: metal or bamboo skewers
(if using bamboo, soak in water for at least
30 minutes)
LEVEL OF SPICINESS: 3/10

Marinade

¼ cup plus 2 tablespoons pineapple juice
3 tablespoons rice vinegar
2 tablespoons molasses *or* black treacle
2 tablespoons hot chilli-garlic sauce, such as
    Sriracha or other hot sauce
2 teaspoons coarse sea salt

800 grams sirloin steak, trimmed of excess fat and
    cut into 2.5 cm cubes
16 pickling onions, 200–240 grams total
8 cherry tomatoes
1 large green pepper, stemmed, deseeded and cut
    into 2.5 cm squares
8 fresh pineapple cubes, each about 2.5 cm square
Vegetable oil
4 cups cooked white rice

1. In a small bowl, whisk the marinade ingredients. Place the meat in a large, resealable plastic bag and pour in the marinade. Press the air out of the bag and seal tightly. Massage the bag to distribute the marinade. Refrigerate for 4–6 hours, turning once or twice.

2. With a sharp knife make an 'x' on the tip of each onion. Bring a small saucepan of water to a boil; immerse the onions and simmer for 5 minutes. Drain and rinse under cold running water. When cool enough to handle, slip off the skins. Refrigerate, covered, until ready to thread the skewers.

3. Prepare the braai for direct cooking over medium-high heat 200°–260°C (400°–500°F).

4. Remove the meat from the bag and reserve the marinade. Pour the marinade into a small saucepan and boil for one full minute. Set aside for basting the kebabs. Thread the meat, onions, tomatoes, green pepper and pineapple onto the skewers, distributing them as evenly as possible. Brush lightly all over with oil.

5. Brush the cooking grates clean. Braai the kebabs over ***direct medium-high heat***, with the lid closed as much as possible, until cooked to your desired doneness, 6–8 minutes for medium rare, turning once or twice and basting with the boiled marinade once after 4 minutes. Serve right away with the rice.

Serving suggestion: Brown Rice Salad with Lime Dressing (for recipe, see page 133).

SERVES: 4

PORTERHOUSE STEAKS
WITH BRANDY BLACK PEPPER BUTTER

PREP TIME: 20 minutes
BRAAIING TIME: 6 to 8 minutes
SPECIAL EQUIPMENT: long match
LEVEL OF SPICINESS: 2/10

4 porterhouse steaks, each about 450 grams and
    2.5 cm thick, trimmed of excess fat
2 tablespoons extra-virgin olive oil
1½ teaspoons coarse sea salt
¾ teaspoon ground black pepper

Butter

2 tablespoons cold, unsalted butter
2 tablespoons finely chopped shallot
¼ cup plus 1 teaspoon brandy, divided
¼ cup (60 g) unsalted butter, softened
1 tablespoon finely chopped fresh chives
1 tablespoon coarsely ground black pepper
2 teaspoons finely chopped fresh thyme leaves
½ teaspoon coarse sea salt

NOTE!

Serve the steaks with braaied new potatoes,
if desired. Cut the potatoes in half or quarter,
coat with oil and season with salt and pepper.
Braai over *direct medium heat*, with the lid
closed, until they are tender and browned on
all sides, 15–20 minutes, turning occasionally.

1. Brush the steaks on both sides with the oil and
season evenly with the salt and pepper. Leave the
steaks to stand at room temperature for 30 minutes
before braaiing.

2. Prepare the braai for direct cooking over high heat
230°–290°C (450°–550°F).

3. In a small pan (with a lid) over medium-high heat,
melt the cold butter. When the foam subsides, add the
shallot and cook until the edges just begin to brown
slightly, about 2 minutes, stirring occasionally.
Remove the pan from the heat and add ¼ cup of
the brandy. Using a long match, carefully ignite the
brandy (the flames will rise high above the pan, so be
careful), return the pan over medium-high heat, and
let it burn for 30 seconds. If the brandy does not
extinguish itself, cover the pan tightly with the lid.
Transfer the mixture to a bowl and let cool.

4. In a separate bowl, combine the softened butter,
chives, pepper, thyme and salt. Add the cooled shallot
mixture and the remaining 1 teaspoon brandy,
stirring well to combine. Keep at room temperature.

5. Brush the cooking grates clean. Braai the steaks over
direct high heat, with the lid closed as much as possible,
until cooked to your desired doneness, 6–8 minutes
for medium rare, turning once or twice (if flare-ups
occur, move the steaks temporarily over indirect heat).
Remove from the braai and let rest for 3–5 minutes.

6. Serve the steaks warm with the butter mixture
spooned over the top.

SERVES: 4 to 6

SMOKY RED HOT T-BONE STEAKS
WITH TOMATO-CHILLI SALSA

PREP TIME: 20 minutes
BRAAIING TIME: 12 to 14 minutes
SPECIAL EQUIPMENT: 2 handfuls mesquite wood chips, soaked in water for at least 30 minutes; rubber gloves
LEVEL OF SPICINESS: 7/10

Rub

2 habanero chilli peppers, preferably red
2 tablespoons extra-virgin olive oil
1 teaspoon coarse sea salt
1 teaspoon coarsely ground black pepper
1 garlic clove, finely chopped

3 T-bone steaks, each about 560 grams and
      2.5 cm thick, trimmed of excess fat
Extra-virgin olive oil

Salsa

2 slices onion, each about 1.5 cm thick
5-6 red chilli peppers, such as Thai, stems removed
2 large tomatoes
⅓ cup roughly chopped fresh coriander leaves
Juice of 1 lime, divided
½ teaspoon coarse sea salt
¼ teaspoon coarsely ground black pepper

1. Wearing rubber gloves (to avoid burning your skin), remove and discard the stems and seeds from the habaneros. Mince or finely chop the habaneros. In a small bowl, combine the rub ingredients.

Lightly brush the steaks on both sides with oil, season evenly with the rub and leave to stand at room temperature for 15–30 minutes before braaiing.

2. Prepare the braai for direct cooking over high heat 230°–290°C (450°–550°F).

3. Brush the cooking grates clean. Lightly brush the onion slices on both sides with oil. Braai the chilli peppers, tomatoes and onion slices over *direct high heat*, with the lid closed as much as possible, until the chillies and the tomatoes are blackened and blistered all over and the onions are tender, about 6 minutes, turning occasionally. Remove from the braai and leave to cool.

4. Core the tomatoes and coarsely chop them. Cut the onions and chillies into large pieces. Put the tomatoes, onions and chillies into a food processor and pulse into a coarse paste. Transfer the mixture to a bowl and stir in the coriander, half the lime juice, the salt and the pepper.

5. Brush the cooking grates clean. Drain the wood chips and add them to the charcoal or to the smoker box of a gas braai, following manufacturer's instructions, and close the lid. When the wood begins to smoke, braai the steaks over *direct high heat*, with the lid closed as much as possible, until cooked to your desired doneness, 6–8 minutes for medium rare, turning once or twice. Transfer the steaks to a platter and leave to rest for 3–5 minutes. Drizzle the remaining lime juice over the steaks, and serve with the salsa on the side.

SERVES: 6

CHARRED CHILLI BEEF KEBABS
WITH GUACAMOLE

PREP TIME: 25 minutes
MARINATING TIME: 2 to 4 hours
CHILLING TIME: up to 1 hour
BRAAIING TIME: 6 to 8 minutes
SPECIAL EQUIPMENT: 6 metal or bamboo skewers (if using bamboo, soak in water for at least 30 minutes), rubber gloves
LEVEL OF SPICINESS: 6/10

Marinade
3 large jalapeño chilli peppers
1 habanero chilli pepper
1 medium onion, finely chopped
1 cup beer
½ cup roughly chopped fresh coriander leaves
¼ cup fresh lime juice
4 garlic cloves, finely chopped

Coarse sea salt
Ground black pepper
1.5 kg sirloin, about 3 cm thick, trimmed of
    excess fat, cut into 3 cm cubes

Guacamole
2 ripe avocados
1 medium tomato, cored, seeded and finely chopped
1 medium jalapeño chilli pepper, seeded and
    finely chopped
2 tablespoons roughly chopped fresh coriander leaves
1 tablespoon fresh lime juice
1 small garlic clove, crushed or very finely chopped

Extra-virgin olive oil

1. Put the jalapeños over a gas burner set to medium heat, or under the grill, and char the skins all over, 4–6 minutes, turning as needed. Transfer to a cutting board and, when cool enough to handle, finely chop them. Wearing rubber gloves (to avoid burning your skin), remove and discard the stem and seeds from the habanero and chop very finely. Combine the marinade ingredients, including 1½ teaspoons salt and ½ teaspoon pepper. Add the meat cubes and turn to coat. Cover and refrigerate for 2–4 hours.

2. In a bowl, mash the avocados with the back of a fork. Stir in the remaining guacamole ingredients, including 2 tablespoons oil, ½ teaspoon salt and ⅛ teaspoon pepper. Place a piece of cling wrap directly on the surface of the guacamole to prevent it from browning, and refrigerate for up to 1 hour.

3. Prepare the braai for direct cooking over high heat 230°–290°C (450°–550°F).

4. Remove the meat from the bowl and pat dry (it's okay if there are bits of pepper, onion or coriander clinging to it). Discard the marinade. Wearing rubber gloves, thread the meat onto the skewers, leaving a little space between each piece. Brush lightly on all sides with oil.

5. Brush the cooking grates clean. Braai the kebabs over **direct high heat**, with the lid closed as much as possible, until dark, caramelized and cooked to your desired doneness, 6–8 minutes for medium rare, turning once or twice. Remove from the braai, season with salt, and serve warm with the guacamole.

SERVES: 6

MUSTARD PRIME RIB
WITH HORSERADISH CREAM

PREP TIME: 20 minutes
MARINATING TIME: 12 to 24 hours
BRAAIING TIME: 2¾ to 3 hours
SPECIAL EQUIPMENT: spice mill,
instant-read thermometer
LEVEL OF SPICINESS: 3/10

Paste
2 tablespoons whole black peppercorns
2 tablespoons mustard seeds
½ cup country-style wholegrain mustard
2 tablespoons Worcestershire sauce
2 tablespoons chopped fresh rosemary leaves

1 'seven-bone' prime rib roast (5–6 kg), trimmed
    of excess fat

Cream
1 cup sour cream
2 tablespoons prepared horseradish
1 tablespoon dried green peppercorns, crushed
1 tablespoon Worcestershire sauce

2 tablespoons coarse sea salt

1. Crush the peppercorns and the mustard seeds in a spice mill. Transfer to a small bowl and combine with the remaining paste ingredients.

2. Spread the paste evenly all over the roast, cover with cling wrap, and refrigerate for 12–24 hours. Leave the roast to stand at room temperature for 30–40 minutes before braaiing.

3. Prepare the braai for indirect cooking over medium heat 180°–230°C (350°–450°F).

4. In a small bowl, whisk the cream ingredients. Refrigerate until ready to serve.

5. Brush the cooking grates clean. Season the roast evenly with the salt, and braai over ***indirect medium heat***, with the lid closed, until an instant-read thermometer inserted into the thickest part of the roast registers 55°–60°C for medium rare, 2¾–3 hours. Start checking the temperature of the roast after 2½ hours. Keep the braai's temperature between 180° and 190°C (350°–375°F).

6. Remove the roast from the braai, loosely cover with foil, and leave to rest for 20–30 minutes (the internal temperature of the meat will rise by 5–10 degrees during this time).

7. Using a sharp knife, remove the bones from the roast and cut the meat into 2 cm slices. Serve warm with the horseradish cream on the side.

SERVES: 12 to 15

THAI-MARINATED FLANK STEAK
WITH SAMBAL OLEK

PREP TIME: 15 minutes
MARINATING TIME: 4 to 24 hours
BRAAIING TIME: 8 to 10 minutes
LEVEL OF SPICINESS: 4/10

Marinade

3 tablespoons fresh lime juice
2 tablespoons fish sauce
2 tablespoons vegetable oil
1 tablespoon sugar
1 tablespoon *sambal olek*
1 tablespoon red curry paste
1 tablespoon grated fresh ginger
1 tablespoon crushed garlic

1 flank steak, 700–900 grams and about 2 cm thick

Sauce

¼ cup fresh lime juice
2 tablespoons *sambal olek*
2 tablespoons finely chopped fresh coriander leaves
2 teaspoons sugar
2 teaspoons fish sauce
2 teaspoons water

1. In a medium bowl, whisk the marinade ingredients. Put the steak into a large glass dish and pour in the marinade. Turn to coat both sides. Cover with cling wrap and refrigerate for at least 4 hours or up to 24 hours. Remove the steak from the marinade, letting the excess drip back into the dish. Discard the marinade. Leave the steak to stand at room temperature for 15–30 minutes before braaiing.

2. Prepare the braai for direct cooking over medium heat 180º–230ºC (350º–450ºF).

3. In a small bowl, whisk the sauce ingredients.

4. Brush the cooking grates clean. Braai the steak over **direct medium heat**, with the lid closed as much as possible, until cooked to your desired doneness, 8–10 minutes for medium rare, turning once or twice (if flare-ups occur, move the steak temporarily over indirect heat). Remove from the braai and leave to rest for 3–5 minutes.

5. Cut the steak across the grain into thin slices. Serve warm with the sauce.

SERVES: 4 to 6

NOTE!

Serve the flank steak with grilled green beans, if desired. Preheat a perforated grill pan over *direct medium heat*. Oil the green beans and season with salt and pepper. When the pan is hot, spread the beans in a single layer on the grill pan and braai until they are browned in spots and crisp-tender, 5–7 minutes, turning occasionally.

SPICY BEEF SATAY
WITH COCONUT-PEANUT DIPPING SAUCE

PREP TIME: 30 minutes
MARINATING TIME: 1 to 4 hours
BRAAIING TIME: about 4 minutes
SPECIAL EQUIPMENT: metal or wood skewers
(if using wood, soak in water for 30 minutes)
LEVEL OF SPICINESS: 7/10

Marinade
1 large shallot, coarsely chopped
4 Thai (Bird's-eye) chillies, seeded and coarsely
  chopped *or* 3 tablespoons hot chilli-garlic sauce,
  such as Sriracha
2 tablespoons packed treacle sugar
2 tablespoons peanut *or* canola oil
2 tablespoons water
1 piece fresh ginger, about 2.5 cm, peeled and
  coarsely chopped
1 tablespoon medium curry powder
4 garlic cloves
2 teaspoons grated fresh lime zest
1 teaspoon fish sauce

1 flank steak, 400–500 grams and 2 cm thick
½ teaspoon coarse sea salt

Sauce
¾ cup coconut milk
½ cup crunchy peanut butter
2 tablespoons packed treacle sugar
2 tablespoons fresh lime juice
1 tablespoon fish sauce
1 teaspoon hot chilli-garlic sauce, like Sriracha
¾ teaspoon red curry paste
¼ teaspoon crushed chilli flakes

1. In a food processor or blender, purée the marinade ingredients until combined.

2. Cut the flank steak across the grain into pieces 1.5 cm wide and 10–15 cm long. Place the beef in a bowl, pour in the marinade, and toss to coat. Cover with cling wrap and refrigerate for at least 1 hour or up to 4 hours.

3. Prepare the braai for direct cooking over medium heat 180°–230°C (350°–450°F).

4. In a medium saucepan, combine the sauce ingredients (you will warm the sauce after you have braaied the beef satay).

5. Remove the beef from the refrigerator and discard the marinade. Thread the beef onto the skewers, and season with the salt. Brush the cooking grates clean. Braai over **direct medium heat**, with the lid closed as much as possible, until cooked to your desired doneness, about 4 minutes for medium rare, turning once. Remove from the braai and leave to rest while you warm the sauce.

6. Place the saucepan with the sauce over medium heat and bring to a simmer. Continue cooking until slightly thickened, 2–3 minutes, whisking often. Remove from the heat.

7. Serve the beef satay warm with the dipping sauce.

SERVES: 4 to 6 as an appetizer

PEPPER SKIRT STEAK
WITH DAIKON-ORANGE RELISH

PREP TIME: 20 minutes
MARINATING TIME: 4 to 6 hours
BRAAIING TIME: 4 to 6 minutes
LEVEL OF SPICINESS: 5/10

Marinade

Juice of 2 oranges
1 large jalapeño chilli, finely chopped, with seeds
2 tablespoons extra-virgin olive oil
1 tablespoon fresh lime juice
4 garlic cloves, crushed
1 teaspoon ground black pepper
1 teaspoon coarse sea salt
1 teaspoon Tabasco sauce

700 grams skirt steak, about 2 cm thick, trimmed
    of excess surface fat, cut across into
    25-cm-long pieces

Relish

2 oranges, peeled, seeded and cut into 0.5-cm dice
200 g daikon radish, peeled and cut into 0.5-cm dice
⅓ cup roughly chopped fresh Italian parsley leaves
1 tablespoon extra-virgin olive oil
2 teaspoons fresh lime juice
¼ teaspoon coarse sea salt
¼ teaspoon ground black pepper

1. In a large bowl, combine the marinade ingredients. Place the steak in the bowl, and turn to coat evenly. Cover and refrigerate for 4–6 hours, turning occasionally.

2. Prepare the braai for direct cooking over high heat 230º–290ºC (450º–550ºF).

3. Combine the relish ingredients and refrigerate until shortly before serving time.

4. Brush the cooking grates clean. Lift the steaks from the marinade and let the excess drip back into the bowl. Discard the marinade. Braai the steaks over ***direct high heat***, with the lid closed as much as possible, until cooked to your desired doneness, 4–6 minutes for medium rare, turning once or twice. Remove the steaks from the braai and leave to rest for 3–5 minutes.

5. Cut the steaks across the grain into thin slices and serve warm with the relish.
Serving suggestion: Smoky New Potatoes with Spicy Aïoli (for recipe, see page 131).

SERVES: 4

THAI BEEF SALAD
WITH CASHEWS

PREP TIME: 20 minutes
MARINATING TIME: 30 minutes to 1 hour
BRAAIING TIME: 4 to 6 minutes
LEVEL OF SPICINESS: 6/10

Marinade
2 tablespoons canola oil
2 tablespoons crushed garlic
2 tablespoons hot chilli-garlic sauce, such as Sriracha
1 tablespoon fish sauce

450 grams skirt steak, about 2 cm thick, trimmed of
    surface fat, cut into three 20-cm-long pieces

Dressing
¼ cup fresh lime juice
2–4 Thai (Bird's-eye) chillies, seeded and finely
    chopped *or* ¾–1 teaspoon Thai red curry paste
2 tablespoons plus 1 teaspoon sugar
2 tablespoons fish sauce

Salad
8 cups tightly packed mixed micro greens
1 English cucumber, halved lengthways and thinly
    sliced across
1 red pepper, thinly sliced
½ red onion, halved lengthways and thinly sliced
⅔ cup lightly salted, roasted cashews, chopped
⅓ cup fresh coriander leaves, coarsely chopped
⅓ cup fresh mint leaves, coarsely chopped

1. In a medium bowl, whisk the marinade ingredients. Place the steaks in the bowl, and turn to coat with the marinade. Leave the steaks to marinate at room temperature for 30–60 minutes before braaiing.

2. Prepare the braai for direct cooking over high heat 230°–290°C (450°–550°F).

3. In a small bowl, whisk the dressing ingredients. In a large bowl, toss the salad ingredients.

4. Brush the cooking grates clean. Braai the steak over **direct high heat**, with the lid closed as much as possible, until cooked to your desired doneness, 4–6 minutes for medium rare, turning once or twice (if flare-ups occur, move the steaks temporarily over indirect heat). Remove from the braai and leave to rest for 3–5 minutes.

5. Pour the dressing over the salad and toss to coat. Divide the salad evenly among four plates. Cut the steak across the grain into thin slices. Top each salad with the steak and serve immediately.

SERVES: 4

BUTTERFLIED LEG OF LAMB
WITH AROMATIC SPICE RUB AND DRIED CHERRY CHUTNEY

PREP TIME: 10 minutes, plus about
40 minutes for the chutney
BRAAIING TIME: 30 to 45 minutes
LEVEL OF SPICINESS: 6/10

Chutney

2 tablespoons extra-virgin olive oil
2 large shallots, finely chopped (about 1 cup)
1 tablespoon peeled, grated fresh ginger
1 tablespoon crushed garlic
1 teaspoon ground cumin
1 teaspoon ground coriander
¾ teaspoon crushed red chilli flakes
¼ teaspoon ground cinnamon
2 cups dried tart cherries or dried cranberries
1 cup red wine vinegar
¾ cup sugar
½ teaspoon coarse sea salt

Rub

1 tablespoon ground cumin
1 tablespoon coarse sea salt
2 teaspoons ground coriander
1 teaspoon ground ginger
1 teaspoon garlic powder
1 teaspoon dried origanum
1 teaspoon ground cayenne pepper
¾ teaspoon ground cinnamon

1 deboned leg of lamb, 1.3–1.5 kg, butterflied and
    trimmed of excess fat
Extra-virgin olive oil

1. In a medium saucepan over medium heat, warm the oil. Add the shallots, ginger and garlic, and cook until the shallots start to soften, about 2 minutes, stirring occasionally. Stir in the cumin, coriander, crushed red chilli flakes and cinnamon, and cook until fragrant, about 30 seconds. Add the cherries, vinegar and sugar. Increase the heat to medium-high and bring the mixture to a boil. Reduce the heat to medium and simmer until thickened, 30–35 minutes, stirring occasionally. Remove from the heat and stir in the salt.

2. In a small bowl, combine the rub ingredients. Brush the lamb all over with oil and season evenly with the rub. Leave the lamb to stand at room temperature for about 30 minutes before braaiing.

3. Prepare the braai for direct and indirect cooking over medium heat 180°–230°C (350°–450°F).

4. Brush the cooking grates clean. Sear the lamb, fat side up first, over ***direct medium heat***, with the lid closed as much as possible, until nicely browned on both sides, 10–15 minutes, turning once or twice. Slide the lamb over ***indirect medium heat***, close the lid, and cook to your desired doneness, 20–30 minutes more for medium rare. Remove from the braai and leave to rest for 5–10 minutes.

5. Cut the lamb across the grain into 0.5 cm slices and serve warm with the chutney.

SERVES: 6 to 8

LAMB KEBABS
WITH ZHOUG DIPPING SAUCE

PREP TIME: 30 minutes
MARINATING TIME: 4 to 24 hours
BRAAIING TIME: 20 to 25 minutes
SPECIAL EQUIPMENT: 6 metal or wood skewers
(if using wood, soak in water for 30 minutes)
LEVEL OF SPICINESS: 10/10

¼ cup extra-virgin olive oil
2 tablespoons fresh lemon juice
3 large garlic cloves, crushed
2½ teaspoons coarse sea salt, divided
1 teaspoon ground black pepper, divided
1 teaspoon ground cumin, divided
½ teaspoon ground coriander
½ teaspoon ground cayenne pepper
½ teaspoon ground cinnamon
¼ teaspoon ground nutmeg
¼ teaspoon ground cloves
1.2 kg deboned leg of lamb, trimmed of excess fat
    and cut into 4 cm cubes

Sauce
1 medium green pepper
½ cup tightly packed fresh coriander leaves and
    tender stems
½ cup tightly packed fresh Italian parsley leaves and
    tender stems
6 green Thai (Bird's-eye) chillies, stemmed and
    deseeded
1 tablespoon fresh lemon juice
2 large garlic cloves, crushed
3 tablespoons extra-virgin olive oil, divided

1. In a small bowl, whisk the oil, lemon juice, garlic, 2 teaspoons salt, ½ teaspoon black pepper, ½ teaspoon cumin, the coriander, cayenne pepper, cinnamon, nutmeg and cloves. Place the lamb in a large resealable plastic bag and pour in the marinade. Press the air out of the bag and seal tightly. Turn the bag to distribute the marinade and place in a bowl. Refrigerate for 4 hours or up to 24 hours.

2. Prepare the braai for direct cooking over medium-high heat 200°–260°C (400°–500°F).

3. Brush the cooking grates clean. Braai the green pepper over *direct medium-high heat*, with the lid closed for 12–15 minutes, turning occasionally, until blackened and blistered all over. Place the pepper in a bowl and cover with cling wrap to trap the steam. Leave to stand for about 10 minutes, then remove the pepper and peel away and discard the charred skin, stem and seeds. Transfer to a food processor. Add all the remaining sauce ingredients, except the oil and the remaining salt, black pepper and cumin. Process to blend. Add the oil, 1 tablespoon at a time, to achieve a slightly thick and chunky consistency.

4. Remove the lamb from the bag, and discard the marinade. Allow the lamb to stand at room temperature for 15–30 minutes before braaiing. Thread the lamb onto skewers (approximately 4 cubes per skewer). Brush the cooking grates clean. Braai the lamb skewers over *direct medium-high heat*, with the lid closed, until cooked to your desired doneness, 8–10 minutes for medium rare, turning once or twice. Serve warm with the dipping sauce.

SERVES: 4 to 6

CHILLI-RUBBED LAMB KEBABS
WITH SPICY TOMATO SAUCE

PREP TIME: 15 minutes, plus about 20 minutes
for the sauce
MARINATING TIME: 1 hour
BRAAIING TIME: 8 to 10 minutes
SPECIAL EQUIPMENT: 6 metal or wood skewers
(if using wood, soak in water for 30 minutes)
LEVEL OF SPICINESS: 6/10

Paste
¼ cup vegetable oil
2 tablespoons prepared chilli powder
2 tablespoons ground cumin
4 teaspoons coarse sea salt
2 teaspoons garlic powder
2 teaspoons onion powder

1.2 kg deboned leg of lamb, trimmed of excess fat
and cut into 4 cm cubes

Sauce
1 tablespoon vegetable oil
½ cup finely chopped onion
½ teaspoon crushed garlic
1 can (410 grams) crushed tomatoes in juice
½ teaspoon ground cumin
½ teaspoon prepared chilli powder
1 teaspoon sugar
1 teaspoon tomato paste
½ canned chipotle chilli pepper in adobo sauce
½ teaspoon coarse sea salt
¼ teaspoon dried thyme
¼ teaspoon dried origanum

1. In a large bowl, combine the paste ingredients. Place the lamb cubes in the bowl with the paste and stir to coat evenly. Cover with cling wrap and refrigerate for 1 hour. Meanwhile, make the sauce.

2. In a large sauté pan over medium-high heat, warm the oil. Add the onion and cook until soft, about 4 minutes, stirring occasionally. Stir in the garlic and cook for 1 minute more. Add the tomatoes, including the juice, the cumin and the chilli powder, and bring the mixture to a boil. Reduce the heat to a simmer, and add the remaining sauce ingredients. Cook until almost all of the liquid has evaporated, 10–15 minutes, stirring occasionally. Transfer the mixture to a food processor and process until smooth. Return the sauce to the sauté pan. Set aside.

3. Leave the lamb to stand at room temperature for 15–30 minutes before braaiing.

4. Prepare the braai for direct cooking over high heat 230°–290°C (450°–550°F).

5. Thread the lamb onto skewers (approximately 4 cubes per skewer), leaving a little room between each piece. Brush the cooking grates clean. Braai the kebabs over *direct high heat*, with the lid closed as much as possible, until cooked to your desired doneness, 8–10 minutes for medium rare, turning once. Meanwhile, reheat the sauce over low heat. Serve the lamb hot with the sauce.

SERVES: 4 to 6

SPICY LAMB MEATBALL PITAS
WITH YOGHURT SAUCE

PREP TIME: 40 minutes
CHILLING TIME: 2 to 4 hours
BRAAIING TIME: 8 to 10 minutes
SPECIAL EQUIPMENT: spice mill or mortar and pestle
LEVEL OF SPICINESS: 8/10

Spicy lamb meatballs

2 teaspoons cumin seeds
1 teaspoon fennel seeds
1 teaspoon coriander seeds
900 grams lamb mince
⅓ cup harissa paste (from a can or a jar)
1 tablespoon crushed garlic
1½ teaspoons coarse sea salt
1 teaspoon ground cayenne pepper

Sauce

2 cups thick Greek yoghurt
¼ cup fresh lemon juice
2 tablespoons finely chopped fresh mint leaves
2 teaspoons crushed garlic
½ teaspoon coarse sea salt

Extra-virgin olive oil
6–8 pita breads
3 cups halved cherry tomatoes
1 bunch fresh mint, roughly chopped
1 bunch fresh coriander, roughly chopped

1. In a small pan over medium heat, toast the cumin seeds, fennel seeds and coriander seeds until fragrant, about 1 minute, shaking the pan constantly. Transfer to a spice mill and finely grind.

2. In a large bowl, combine the toasted spices with the remaining meatball ingredients, mixing with a fork. Do not overwork the meat or it will be tough. With wet hands, form the mixture into equal-sized balls, each about 4 cm in diameter, and flatten them slightly (you will have 40–44 meatballs). Place the meatballs on a baking tray, cover with cling wrap and refrigerate for 2–4 hours.

3. Prepare the braai for direct cooking over medium heat 180°–230°C (350°–450°F).

4. In a small bowl, whisk the sauce ingredients. Refrigerate until ready to serve.

5. Brush the cooking grates clean. Lightly brush the meatballs all over with oil. Braai over ***direct medium heat***, with the lid closed as much as possible, until fully cooked, 8–10 minutes, turning occasionally. During the last 1–2 minutes of braaiing time, warm the pita breads over direct heat, turning once or twice.

6. Cut each pita bread in two, and place three meatballs in each pita half. Spoon some yoghurt sauce over the meatballs, along with the tomatoes and herbs. Serve right away.

SERVES: 6 to 8

GINGER CURRY LAMB CHOPS

WITH YOGHURT SAUCE

PREP TIME: 20 minutes
MARINATING TIME: 2 to 4 hours
BRAAIING TIME: 8 to 10 minutes
LEVEL OF SPICINESS: 3/10

Sauce

½ cup thick Greek yoghurt
1 tablespoon finely chopped fresh coriander leaves
2 teaspoons fresh lime juice
1 teaspoon chilli-garlic paste
½ small garlic clove, crushed
¼ teaspoon coarse sea salt
⅛ teaspoon garam masala

Marinade

3 tablespoons fresh lime juice
2 tablespoons finely grated fresh ginger
2 tablespoons extra-virgin olive oil
2 teaspoons Madras curry powder
1 teaspoon smoked paprika
1 teaspoon ground turmeric
1 teaspoon ground cayenne pepper
1 teaspoon coarse sea salt
1 teaspoon ground black pepper

8 thick-cut lamb loin chops (each about 4 cm thick),
    trimmed of excess fat

1. In a small bowl, whisk the sauce ingredients. Cover with cling wrap and refrigerate until 30 minutes before serving.

2. In a small bowl, whisk the marinade ingredients. Place the lamb chops in a large glass baking dish and pour the marinade over them, turning to coat. Cover with cling wrap and refrigerate for at least 2 hours or up to 4 hours. Leave the chops to stand at room temperature for 15–30 minutes before braaiing.

3. Prepare the braai for direct cooking over medium heat 180°–230°C (350°–450°F).

4. Remove the chops from the dish and discard the marinade. Brush the cooking grates clean. Braai the chops over *direct medium heat*, with the lid closed as much as possible, until cooked to your desired doneness, 8–10 minutes for medium rare, turning once. Remove the chops from the braai and leave to rest for 3–5 minutes. Serve the chops warm with the yoghurt sauce on the side.

SERVES: 4

MARINATED LAMB RACKS
WITH RHUBARB-HORSERADISH CHUTNEY

PREP TIME: 40 minutes
MARINATING TIME: 4 to 12 hours
BRAAIING TIME: 20 to 27 minutes
LEVEL OF SPICINESS: 5/10

Paste
¾ cup thick Greek yoghurt
Juice of ½ lime
1 teaspoon ground cayenne pepper
1 teaspoon paprika
1 teaspoon ground turmeric
1 teaspoon ground cumin
1 teaspoon ground cardamom
1 teaspoon ground black pepper
½ teaspoon mustard powder
½ teaspoon ground cinnamon

Coarse sea salt
2 racks of lamb (8 ribs), each ± 800 grams, frenched

Chutney
4 large stalks rhubarb (± 450 grams), cut into
    1.5-cm pieces, divided
⅔ cup sugar
½ cup finely chopped red onion
½ cup sultanas *or* dried cranberries
¼ cup red wine vinegar
Finely grated zest and juice of ½ orange
1 small Thai (Bird's-eye) chilli, finely chopped
1 tablespoon peeled, crushed fresh ginger
2 tablespoons prepared horseradish
3 tablespoons chopped fresh mint leaves

1. In a small bowl, combine the paste ingredients, including 1 teaspoon salt.

2. Trim any loose fat from the lamb racks and trim the surface fat to 0.5 cm. Spread the paste all over the lamb, completely covering the meat but leaving the bones exposed. Place in a shallow dish, cover with cling wrap and refrigerate for at least 4 hours or up to 12 hours. Leave the lamb to stand at room temperature for about 30 minutes before braaiing.

3. Prepare the braai for direct and indirect cooking over medium heat 180°–230°C (350°–450°F).

4. In a medium saucepan over high heat, combine half the rhubarb with the sugar, onion, sultanas, vinegar, orange zest and juice, chilli, ginger and ½ teaspoon salt. Bring to a boil, and then reduce the heat to medium and simmer until the rhubarb starts

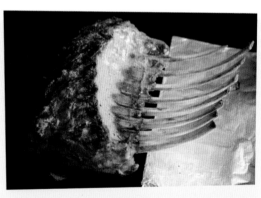

To protect the bones from burning on the braai, place a sheet of foil under them (but not under the meat) while the meat is browning.

to fall apart, about 5 minutes. Add the remaining rhubarb, reduce the heat to medium-low, and cook until the mixture thickens slightly and the rhubarb pieces are tender but still holding their shape, 8–10 minutes more. Remove from the heat and stir in the horseradish. May be kept at room temperature for up to 2 hours, or cover and refrigerate for up to 4 days. Reheat just before serving, and stir in the mint.

5. Brush the cooking grates clean. Braai the lamb over *direct medium heat*, with the lid closed as much as possible, until the meat is browned all over, 10–12 minutes, turning once or twice (watch for flare-ups). Slide the lamb over *indirect medium heat*, close the lid, and cook to your desired doneness, 10–15 minutes more for medium rare. Remove from the braai and leave to rest for 5–10 minutes.

6. Cut the lamb between the bones into individual chops. Place two chops on each plate and drizzle with any accumulated juices. Spoon the warm chutney alongside the chops and serve immediately.

SERVES: 4

CORIANDER PORK BURGERS
WITH SPICY SLAW

PREP TIME: 20 minutes
BRAAIING TIME: 10 to 12 minutes
LEVEL OF SPICINESS: 4/10

Slaw

2½ cups thinly sliced green cabbage
½ cup grated carrots
1 small red onion, very thinly sliced (about ⅓ cup)
⅓ cup mayonnaise
1 tablespoon fresh lime juice
2 teaspoons sugar
¾ teaspoon chipotle chilli powder
½ teaspoon ancho chilli powder
¼ teaspoon coarse sea salt
¼ teaspoon ground black pepper

Patties

700 grams lean pork mince
⅓ cup roughly chopped fresh coriander leaves
1 tablespoon fresh lime juice
1 teaspoon coarse sea salt
½ teaspoon ground black pepper
¼ teaspoon ground cumin

4 hamburger buns, split

1. In a large bowl, mix the slaw ingredients. Cover and refrigerate until ready to serve.

2. Prepare the braai for direct cooking over medium heat 180°–230°C (350°–450°F).

3. In a large bowl, gently combine the patty ingredients. With wet hands, form the mixture into four loosely packed patties of equal size, each about 2 cm thick. Don't compact the meat too much or the patties will be tough. With your thumb or the back of a spoon, make a shallow indentation about 2.5 cm wide in the centre of each patty. This will help the patties cook evenly and prevent them from puffing up on the braai.

4. Brush the cooking grates clean. Braai the patties over ***direct medium heat***, with the lid closed as much as possible, until firm and fully cooked but still moist, 10–12 minutes, turning once when the patties release easily from the grate without sticking (if flare-ups occur, move the patties temporarily over indirect heat). During the last minute of braaiing time, toast the buns, cut side down, over direct heat.

5. Serve the patties hot on the toasted buns, topped with the slaw.

SERVES: 4

SPICY PORK MEATBALL SLIDERS

PREP TIME: 1 hour
CHILLING TIME: 2 hours
BRAAIING TIME: 8 to 10 minutes
LEVEL OF SPICINESS: 8/10

Meatballs

2 tablespoons ricotta cheese
1 large egg
700 grams lean pork mince
½ cup drained and finely chopped Peppadews
    (hot cherry peppers)
½ cup fine breadcrumbs
¼ cup freshly grated Parmesan-style cheese
¼ cup finely chopped fresh Italian parsley leaves
3 garlic cloves, crushed
1 teaspoon paprika
1 teaspoon dried origanum
1 teaspoon coarse sea salt
1 teaspoon ground black pepper
½ teaspoon crushed red chilli flakes

Sauce

1 tablespoon extra-virgin olive oil
1 medium onion, finely chopped (about 1 cup)
2 medium garlic cloves, crushed
1 teaspoon crushed red chilli flakes
½ teaspoon dried origanum
2 cans (800 grams) crushed Italian plum tomatoes
2 tablespoons tomato paste
1 teaspoon coarse sea salt

Extra-virgin olive oil
12 slider buns or small, soft dinner rolls, split
12 large fresh basil leaves

1. In a small bowl, whisk the ricotta and the egg. In a large bowl, combine the remaining meatball ingredients. Pour the ricotta-egg mixture into the large bowl and gently mix the meatball ingredients with a fork. With wet hands, form the mixture into twelve 5-cm balls and flatten them slightly. Cover with cling wrap and refrigerate for 2 hours.

2. In a large pan over medium heat, warm the oil. Add the onion and sauté until tender but not golden, about 3 minutes. Add the garlic, chilli flakes and origanum. Cook until fragrant, about 1 minute, stirring often. Add the tomatoes, tomato paste and salt. Simmer, partially covered, for about 30 minutes. Remove from the heat and cover to keep warm.

3. Prepare the braai for direct cooking over medium heat 180°–230°C (350°–450°F).

4. Brush the cooking grates clean. Lightly brush the meatballs and the cut sides of the buns with oil. Braai the meatballs over *direct medium heat*, with the lid closed as much as possible, until cooked through, 8–10 minutes, turning two or three times. During the last 30 seconds of braaiing time, toast the buns, cut side down, over direct heat. Transfer the meatballs to the pan with the sauce. Simmer over medium-low heat to heat through.

5. To assemble the sliders: Use a spoon to scoop up one meatball with some sauce, and place it on a bottom bun half. Top with a basil leaf. Place a top bun half over the basil, and secure with a toothpick. Repeat with the remaining meatballs and buns. Serve immediately.

SERVES: 6 to 12 as an appetizer

PORK BURGERS
SPIKED WITH PEPPERS AND MANGO MUSTARD

PREP TIME: 20 minutes
CHILLING TIME: 30 minutes
BRAAIING TIME: 10 to 12 minutes
LEVEL OF SPICINESS: 5/10

Mango mustard

1 ripe mango, about 700 grams
3 tablespoons spicy brown mustard
2 tablespoons honey
2 teaspoons hot chilli-garlic sauce, such as Sriracha
    or other hot pepper sauce

Patties

700 grams lean pork mince
4 jalapeño chillies, seeded and minced
3 spring onions, trimmed and cut into thin slices
¼ cup mango mustard (*see* recipe above)
1 tablespoon dried green peppercorns, crushed with
    the side of a knife
2 garlic cloves, crushed
½ teaspoon coarse sea salt
½ teaspoon ground black pepper

Vegetable oil
4 soft hamburger buns, split
8 butter lettuce leaves

1. Remove the mango pit by slicing down the length of the fruit on either side of the flat pit; discard the pit. Cut through the flesh of the mango, but not the skin, in a crosshatch pattern, and scoop the flesh from each half with a large spoon. In a food processor, purée the mango flesh and the remaining mango mustard ingredients until smooth. Scrape into a small bowl; set aside.

2. In a large bowl, combine the patty ingredients. Don't overwork the meat or the patties will be tough. With wet hands, gently form four patties of equal size, each about 2 cm thick. Using your thumb or the back of a spoon, make a shallow indentation about 2.5 cm wide in the centre of each patty. This will help the patties cook evenly and prevent them from puffing up on the braai. Refrigerate for 30 minutes to firm them up.

3. Prepare the braai for direct cooking over medium heat 180°–230°C (350°–450°F).

4. Brush the cooking grates clean. Lightly brush both sides of each patty with oil. Braai over *direct medium heat*, with the lid closed as much as possible, until firm and fully cooked but still moist, 10–12 minutes, turning once (if flare-ups occur, move the patties temporarily over indirect heat). During the last minute of braaiing time, toast the buns, cut side down, over direct heat.

5. Build each burger with two lettuce leaves, and serve right away with the remaining mango mustard.

SERVES: 4

SAVOURY PORK SOUVLAKI
WITH GREEK SALAD

PREP TIME: 25 minutes
MARINATING TIME: 6 to 8 hours
BRAAIING TIME: 8 to 10 minutes
SPECIAL EQUIPMENT: metal or wood skewers
(if using wood, soak in water for 30 minutes)
LEVEL OF SPICINESS: 2/10 to 6/10 (depending on
the chilli powder used in the marinade)

Marinade

¼ cup extra-virgin olive oil
2 tablespoons fresh lemon juice
1 teaspoon ground cumin
1 teaspoon dried origanum
1 teaspoon mild or hot chilli powder
1 teaspoon coarse sea salt
¾ teaspoon ground black pepper

1 deboned pork loin, about 700 grams, trimmed of
   excess fat and cut into 2.5-cm chunks

Salad

¼ cup extra-virgin olive oil
1 tablespoon red wine vinegar
2 cups cherry tomatoes, cut into quarters
1 large cucumber, peeled, seeded and cut into
   1.5-cm dice
120 grams feta cheese, cut into 1.5-cm cubes
1 medium or 2 small shallots, cut lengthways
   into slivers

Lemon wedges

1. In a small bowl, whisk the marinade ingredients. Put the pork cubes into a large, resealable plastic bag and pour in the marinade. Press the air out of the bag and seal tightly. Turn the bag to distribute the marinade, place on a plate and refrigerate for 6–8 hours, turning occasionally.

2. Prepare the braai for direct cooking over medium-high heat 200°–230°C (400°–500°F).

3. Remove the pork from the bag and discard the marinade. Thread the pork snugly onto the skewers, dividing it evenly.

4. In a small bowl, whisk the oil and vinegar until emulsified. Fold in the remaining salad ingredients. Refrigerate until serving time.

5. Brush the cooking grates clean. Braai the souvlaki (kebabs) over **direct medium-high heat**, with the lid closed as much as possible, until the outsides are evenly seared and the pork is just barely pink in the centre, 8–10 minutes, making sure all four sides come into contact with the cooking grates. Check the salad for seasoning (if the feta is very salty, it may not need additional salt). Squeeze the lemon wedges over the souvlaki and serve warm with the chilled salad.

SERVES: 4

BEER-SIMMERED BRATS
WITH SPICY ONION RELISH

PREP TIME: 10 minutes, plus about 30 minutes for the relish
BRAAIING TIME: 22 to 23 minutes
SPECIAL EQUIPMENT: large disposable foil tray
LEVEL OF SPICINESS: 4/10

Relish

2 tablespoons unsalted butter
700 grams onions, halved lengthways
    and thinly sliced
3 tablespoons sugar
¾ teaspoon coarse sea salt
1 small green pepper, finely chopped
1 tablespoon crushed garlic
3 tablespoons red wine vinegar
2 teaspoons finely chopped canned chipotle chilli
    pepper in adobo sauce
1 teaspoon adobo sauce (from the can)
1 tablespoon ketchup or tomato purée

Brats

2 cans beer
2 tablespoons spicy brown mustard
2 tablespoons sugar
1 teaspoon caraway seed
8 large bratwurst

8 hot-dog rolls or mini ciabattas, split
Spicy brown mustard (optional)

1. In a large pan over medium-high heat, melt the butter. Add the onions, sugar and salt and cook until the onions are slightly softened, about 6 minutes, stirring occasionally. Stir in the pepper and the garlic, and continue cooking until the onions are golden, 18–20 minutes more, stirring occasionally and reducing the heat as the onions darken. Stir in the vinegar and cook, stirring, until evaporated, 30–45 seconds. Add the chipotle chilli pepper and the adobo sauce and cook for about 2 minutes. Stir in the ketchup or tomato purée and cook for 1 minute more. Remove from the heat.

2. Prepare the braai for direct cooking over high heat 230°–290°C (450°–550°F).

3. Brush the cooking grates clean. In a large disposable foil tray, combine the beer, mustard, sugar and caraway seed. Add the bratwurst, place the pan over ***direct high heat***, and bring the liquid to a simmer. Keep the braai lid closed as much as possible. Continue simmering until the brats are evenly coloured and have lost their raw look, about 20 minutes, turning them occasionally. Remove the brats from the liquid, and braai them over ***direct high heat*** until browned, 2–3 minutes, turning once or twice. During the last 30 seconds to 1 minute of braaiing time, toast the buns, cut side down, over direct heat.

4. Place the brats in the toasted buns and top evenly with the onion relish. Serve with spicy brown mustard, if desired.

SERVES: 8

PORK FILLETS
WITH GREEN CHILLI SAUCE

PREP TIME: 10 minutes, plus about 25 minutes for the sauce
MARINATING TIME: 2 to 4 hours
BRAAIING TIME: 25 to 35 minutes
LEVEL OF SPICINESS: 9/10

Rub

2 teaspoons ground cumin
1 teaspoon coarse sea salt
1 teaspoon chipotle chilli powder
1 teaspoon ground coriander
1 teaspoon ground black pepper
1 teaspoon sugar
½ teaspoon ground cayenne pepper

2 pork fillets, each 450–500 grams, trimmed of silver skin and any excess fat
Vegetable oil

Sauce

2 large green peppers
3 green Thai (Bird's-eye) chillies
1 medium onion, chopped (about 1 cup)
2 garlic cloves, crushed
½ teaspoon ground cumin
1 cup chicken stock
1 cup roughly chopped fresh coriander leaves and tender stems
1 teaspoon coarse sea salt

1. Combine the rub ingredients. Lightly brush the pork all over with oil and season evenly with the rub. Cover and refrigerate for 2–4 hours. Leave the pork to stand at room temperature for 15–30 minutes before braaiing.

2. Prepare the braai for direct cooking over medium heat 180°–230°C (350°–450°F).

3. Brush the cooking grates clean. Braai the green peppers and chillies over *direct medium heat*, with the lid closed, until they are blackened and blistered all over, 10–15 minutes, turning occasionally. Place the peppers and chillies in a bowl, cover with cling wrap to trap the steam, set aside for at least 10 minutes, then peel away and discard the charred skins and seeds. Finely chop the peppers and chillies.

4. In a medium saucepan over medium heat, warm 2 tablespoons oil. Add the onion and cook until soft but not golden, about 3 minutes, stirring occasionally. Add the garlic and cumin. Sauté until the onion turns a light golden colour, about 1 minute more. Add the chicken stock, peppers and chillies. Cover and simmer for about 15 minutes. Transfer the mixture to a food processor, add the coriander, and process until blended. Return the mixture to the saucepan. Season with salt and keep warm. Braai the pork over *direct medium heat*, with the lid closed, until the outsides are evenly seared and the insides are barely pink, 15–20 minutes, turning every 5 minutes. Remove from the braai and leave to rest for 3–5 minutes. Cut into 1.5-cm thick slices. Serve warm with the sauce.

SERVES: 4

PORK AND MANGO SKEWERS
WITH VIETNAMESE DIPPING SAUCE

PREP TIME: 20 minutes
BRAAIING TIME: 8 to 10 minutes
SPECIAL EQUIPMENT: 8 metal or wood skewers
(if using wood, soak in water for at least
30 minutes)
LEVEL OF SPICINESS: 5/10

Sauce
3 tablespoons fresh lime juice
2 tablespoons fish sauce
2 tablespoons sugar
1 teaspoon peeled, grated fresh ginger
1 teaspoon hot chilli-garlic sauce, such as Sriracha

Paste
1 tablespoon vegetable oil
1 teaspoon ground cumin
1 teaspoon coarse sea salt
½ teaspoon ground coriander
½ teaspoon sugar
¼ teaspoon Chinese five spice
¼ teaspoon ground cayenne pepper

700 grams deboned pork loin, cut into 4-cm cubes
4 ripe mangoes, cut into 2.5-cm chunks
6 spring onions (white and light green parts only),
    cut into 2.5-cm pieces

1. In a small bowl, whisk the sauce ingredients.

2. In a medium bowl, combine the paste ingredients. Add the pork to the bowl and turn to coat thoroughly. Leave the pork to stand at room temperature for 10–15 minutes before braaiing.

3. Prepare the braai for direct cooking over high heat 230°–290°C (450°–550°F).

4. Thread the pork, mangoes and spring onions alternately onto skewers, leaving a little space between each ingredient.

5. Brush the cooking grates clean. Braai the skewers over **direct high heat**, with the lid closed as much as possible, until the pork is barely pink in the centre, 8–10 minutes, turning once or twice. Remove the skewers from the braai, place on a platter and spoon about half of the sauce over the top. Serve warm with the remaining sauce on the side.

SERVES: 4

PORK VINDALOO
WITH RAITA

PREP TIME: 20 minutes
MARINATING TIME: 4 to 6 hours
CHILLING TIME: at least 1 hour
BRAAIING TIME: 8 to 10 minutes
SPECIAL EQUIPMENT: 8 metal or wood skewers
(if using wood, soak in water for 30 minutes)
LEVEL OF SPICINESS: 6/10

Marinade

1 small onion
3 tablespoons vegetable oil
2 tablespoons white wine vinegar
1 tablespoon crushed garlic
1 tablespoon peeled, grated fresh ginger
1½ teaspoons ground cumin
1 teaspoon ground cayenne pepper
1 teaspoon ground coriander
1 teaspoon ground turmeric
1 teaspoon sugar
1 teaspoon ground black pepper
½ teaspoon ground cinnamon

Coarse sea salt
2 pork fillets, each 450–500 grams, trimmed of
    silver skin and any excess fat

Raita

½ English cucumber
1 cup plain yoghurt
2 tablespoons finely chopped fresh mint leaves
1 tablespoon fresh lemon juice
½ teaspoon ground cumin
1 small garlic clove, crushed

1. Grate the onion using the large holes of a box grater (you should have about ½ cup, including juices). In a large bowl, combine all the marinade ingredients, including 1 teaspoon salt. Cut the pork fillets into 4-cm cubes. Put the pork cubes into a large, resealable plastic bag and pour in the marinade. Press the air out of the bag and seal tightly. Turn the bag to distribute the marinade and place in a bowl. Refrigerate for 4–6 hours.

2. Seed the cucumber (leaving the skin on) and coarsely grate it using the large holes of a box grater. Wrap the grated cucumber in a clean kitchen towel and squeeze dry. Transfer to a medium bowl. Add the remaining raita ingredients, including ½ teaspoon salt, and stir to combine. Cover and refrigerate for at least 1 hour.

3. Remove the pork from the marinade about 20–30 minutes before braaiing, and discard the marinade.

4. Prepare the braai for direct cooking over medium-high heat 200°–230°C (400°–500°F).

5. Thread the pork onto skewers (approximately four cubes per skewer). Brush the cooking grates clean. Braai the skewers over *direct medium-high heat*, with the lid closed, until the pork is barely pink in the centre, 8–10 minutes, turning once or twice. Remove from the braai and serve warm with the raita.

SERVES: 6

PORK YAKITORI
WITH BRAAIED SWEET POTATOES

PREP TIME: 40 minutes
BRAAIING TIME: 10 to 15 minutes
SPECIAL EQUIPMENT: 6 metal or wood skewers
(if using wood, soak in water for 30 minutes)
LEVEL OF SPICINESS: 5/10

Glaze

½ cup soy sauce
½ cup mirin (sweet rice wine)
¼ cup sake *or* dry sherry
2 tablespoons sugar
3 garlic cloves, coarsely chopped
2 red Thai chillies, seeded and coarsely chopped
2 slices peeled fresh ginger, each about 3-mm thick

1½ teaspoons Maizena dissolved in 1 tablespoon water
700 grams deboned pork loin, preferably from
	the rib end
Vegetable oil
½ teaspoon coarse sea salt
700 grams sweet potatoes, peeled
8 spring onions (white and light green parts only)
2 tablespoons toasted sesame seeds
1 small red Thai chilli, seeded and finely chopped

1. In a saucepan over high heat, bring the glaze
ingredients to a boil, stirring to dissolve the sugar.
Boil until the glaze reduces by half, about 7 minutes.
Stir in the dissolved Maizena and cook until just
thickened, about 30 seconds. (Do not let the glaze
caramelize or get too dark or it will be bitter.) Strain
the glaze into a bowl, discard the solids and let cool.

2. Cut the pork loin into 16 strips, each about
10 cm × 4 cm. Thread two to three pork strips onto
each skewer. Generously brush the pork with oil and
season with the salt. Leave the yakitori to stand at
room temperature for 15–30 minutes before braaiing.

3. Prepare the braai for direct cooking over medium-
high heat 230°–260°C (400°–500°F).

4. Cut the sweet potato into wedges. Bring a large
saucepan of salted water to a boil over high heat.
Add the sweet potatoes and cook until almost tender,
about 5 minutes. Drain, rinse under cold water
and pat dry.

5. Brush the cooking grates clean. Brush the sweet
potatoes and the spring onions all over with oil.
Braai the yakitori, sweet potatoes and spring onions
over **direct medium-high heat**, with the lid closed,
until the pork is still slightly pink in the centre, the
potatoes are tender, and the spring onions are crisp-
tender, turning occasionally and brushing the
yakitori and the potatoes with some of the glaze
during the last 2 minutes of braaiing time. The
yakitori and the potatoes will take 10–15 minutes,
and the spring onions 2–3 minutes. Remove from
the braai as they are done.

6. Serve the yakitori, sweet potatoes and spring
onions warm, drizzled with the remaining glaze and
scattered with the toasted sesame seeds and chopped
fresh chilli.

SERVES: 4

CRISPY SHREDDED PORK IN LETTUCE CUPS
WITH CHILLIES AND LIME

PREP TIME: 30 minutes
MARINATING TIME: 6 to 24 hours
BRAAIING TIME: 4 to 5 hours
SPECIAL EQUIPMENT: large disposable foil tray,
instant-read thermometer
LEVEL OF SPICINESS: 7/10

½ cup sugar
½ cup coarse sea salt
1 deboned pork shoulder roast (Boston butt), about
    1.3 kg, trimmed of excess fat

Spring onion and ginger sauce

8 spring onions (white and light green parts only),
    trimmed and thinly sliced
3 tablespoons grapeseed or canola oil
2 tablespoons peeled, finely grated fresh ginger
2 teaspoons soy sauce
1 teaspoon rice vinegar
¼ teaspoon sugar

Chilli sauce

¼ cup fresh lime juice
¼ cup grapeseed or canola oil
2 tablespoons black bean chilli sauce
1–2 tablespoons hot chilli-garlic sauce, such as
    Sriracha

¼ cup packed brown sugar
1 teaspoon coarse sea salt
4 cups cooked basmati rice
Little Gem, cos or butter lettuce leaves

1. Combine the sugar and salt. Rub the roast all over with the spices. Place the roast in a bowl, cover with cling wrap and refrigerate for 6–24 hours. Allow the roast to stand at room temperature for 1 hour before braaiing. In a bowl, mix the spring onion-ginger sauce ingredients. In another bowl, whisk the chilli sauce ingredients. Cover each sauce and refrigerate until ready to use.

2. Prepare the braai for indirect cooking over medium-low heat 150°–200°C (300°–400°F).

3. Remove the roast from the bowl and discard any accumulated juices. Place the roast in a large disposable foil tray and cook over *indirect medium-low heat*, with the lid closed, basting with pan juices every hour, for 4–5 hours, until an instant-read thermometer inserted into the thickest part of the roast registers 90°–95°C. Remove the roast and the foil tray from the braai, tent the meat with foil and leave to rest for about 20 minutes.

4. Increase the braai temperature to high heat 230°–290°C (450°–550°F). Shred the pork in the foil tray, discarding any large pockets of fat. Toss with the pan juices. Season with the brown sugar and salt. Return to the braai and cook over *indirect high heat*, with the lid closed, until the pork begins to crisp and caramelize, 5–10 minutes, stirring occasionally.

5. Spoon some rice and pork into the lettuce leaves, and top with the sauces. Roll up, and serve right away. Serving suggestion: Spicy Carrot and Daikon Radish Slaw (for recipe, *see* page 127).

SERVES: 6; 12 as an appetizer

SLOW-COOKED PORK CARNITAS

PREP TIME: 20 minutes
BRAAIING TIME: 7 to 8 hours
SPECIAL EQUIPMENT: 4 handfuls hickory wood chips, soaked in water for at least 30 minutes; instant-read thermometer
LEVEL OF SPICINESS: 5/10

Rub

2 teaspoons ancho chilli powder
2 teaspoons ground cumin
2 teaspoons ground coriander
2 teaspoons sugar
2 teaspoons ground cayenne pepper
1 teaspoon ground black pepper

Coarse sea salt
1 bone-in pork shoulder roast (Boston butt), 2.5–3 kg, trimmed of excess fat

Baste

4 canned chipotle chilli peppers in adobo sauce
1 cup Mexican beer
½ cup fresh orange juice
2 tablespoons extra-virgin olive oil
2 tablespoons cider vinegar
2 tablespoons packed light brown sugar
1 teaspoon Tabasco sauce

24 corn or flour tortillas (15 cm)
2 cups ready-made guacamole
2 cups fresh tomato salsa
½ cup crumbled feta or *queso fresco* cheese
½ cup loosely packed fresh coriander leaves

1. In a small bowl, combine the rub ingredients, including 1 tablespoon salt. Coat the surface of the roast evenly with the rub. Leave the roast to stand at room temperature for 30 minutes before cooking.

2. Prepare the braai for indirect cooking over medium-low heat, about 150ºC (300ºF).

3. Brush the cooking grates clean. Drain and add two handfuls of the wood chips to the charcoal or to the smoker box of a gas braai, following manufacturer's instructions, and close the lid. When the wood begins to smoke, cook the roast over *indirect medium-low heat*, with the lid closed, for 5 hours. Drain and add one handful of wood chips to the charcoal or to the smoker box every hour until they're gone. If you're using a charcoal braai, replenish the charcoal as needed to maintain a steady temperature, adding about 8 unlit briquettes every 45 minutes to 1 hour. Leave the lid off the braai for about 5 minutes to help the new briquettes light. Eventually the surface of the roast should turn fairly dark and dry. Meanwhile, prepare the baste.

4. Finely chop the chipotle chilli peppers. In a large saucepan over medium-low heat, whisk all of the baste ingredients, including 2 teaspoons salt. Simmer until the brown sugar is melted.

5. Lay two long sheets of aluminum foil on a work surface, overlapping them by 10 cm. Place the roast in the middle of the sheets. Pour about half the baste over the roast and fold up the sides to create a tightly sealed package (reserve the remaining baste).

Return the roast to the braai and continue to cook over ***indirect medium-low heat***, with the lid closed, until the an instant-read thermometer inserted into the thickest part of the roast (not touching the bone) registers 75°C, 2–3 hours more. Remove from the braai, and leave to rest for 30–60 minutes.

6. When the roast is cool enough to handle, pull the meat apart into shreds, discarding any large pieces of fat. Place the shredded meat in a serving dish.

7. Bring the reserved baste sauce to a boil, then reduce the heat to a simmer for about 3 minutes. Add the shredded meat to the sauce and mix well to coat. Keep warm over low heat.

8. Wrap six tortillas in each of four foil packets. Warm the tortilla packets over indirect heat, 2–5 minutes, turning once. Transfer to a plate and keep warm. Serve the meat warm in the tortillas with guacamole, salsa, feta or *queso fresco*, and coriander.

SERVES: 6 to 8

MUSTARD-GLAZED CHICKEN WINGS

PREP TIME: 10 minutes
BRAAIING TIME: about 20 minutes
LEVEL OF SPICINESS: 3/10

Glaze
¼ cup honey
3 tablespoons spicy brown mustard
1 teaspoon Tabasco sauce

Rub
1½ teaspoons coarse sea salt
1 teaspoon garlic flakes
1 teaspoon onion powder
1 teaspoon mustard powder
¾ teaspoon ground cayenne pepper

1.5 kg chicken wings, each cut in half
    at the joint, wing tips removed

1. Prepare the braai for direct and indirect cooking over medium heat 180°–230°C (350°–450°F).

2. In a small saucepan, combine the glaze ingredients. Cook over medium heat until the mixture comes to a simmer, about 1 minute, stirring occasionally. Remove from the heat.

3. In a large bowl, combine the rub ingredients. Add the chicken wings to the bowl and toss well to coat evenly.

4. Brush the cooking grates clean. Braai the wings over **direct medium heat,** with the lid closed as much as possible, until golden brown, about 10 minutes, turning once or twice. Move the wings over **indirect medium heat** and continue braaiing until the skin is brown and crisp and the meat is no longer pink at the bone, about 10 minutes more. During the last 10 minutes of braaiing time, brush the wings evenly with the glaze twice, turning them each time. Serve warm.

SERVES: 8 as an appetizer

CHICKEN BREASTS
WITH CHIPOTLE-TEQUILA GLAZE AND MELON SALSA

PREP TIME: 30 minutes
MARINATING TIME: 2 to 4 hours
CHILLING TIME: up to 2 hours
BRAAIING TIME: 8 to 12 minutes
LEVEL OF SPICINESS: 6/10

Marinade

½ cup roughly chopped fresh coriander leaves
    and tender stems
½ cup fresh orange juice
¼ cup fresh lime juice
¼ cup silver or gold tequila
2 tablespoons extra-virgin olive oil
2 tablespoons honey
2 tablespoons packed light brown sugar
2 large canned chipotle chilli peppers in adobo sauce
1½ teaspoons prepared chilli powder
1½ teaspoons ground cumin
3 garlic cloves, peeled
1 teaspoon coarse sea salt
½ teaspoon ground black pepper

4 large deboned chicken breasts (with skin)

Salsa

1 cup diced sweet melon
1 cup diced honeydew melon
¼ cup finely chopped red onion, rinsed
2½ tablespoons fresh lime juice
½–1 medium jalapeño chilli, finely chopped, with seeds
½ teaspoon coarse sea salt

⅓ cup roughly chopped fresh coriander leaves

1. In a food processor, combine the marinade ingredients and process until the coriander, chipotle chillies and garlic are finely chopped. Place the chicken in a shallow baking dish. Spoon over ½ cup of the marinade, turning to coat. Cover and refrigerate for 2–4 hours, turning the chicken occasionally. Pour the remaining marinade into a small saucepan.

2. Place the saucepan with the marinade over medium-high heat. Bring to a boil and cook until slightly thickened and reduced to ¾ cup, 3–4 minutes. Transfer ½ cup of the reduced marinade to a bowl and set aside for brushing over the chicken while braaiing. Reserve the remaining ¼ cup for serving. Combine the salsa ingredients and toss to blend. Refrigerate for up to 2 hours.

3. Prepare the braai for direct cooking over medium heat 180°–230°C (350°–450°F).

4. Brush the cooking grates clean. Remove the chicken from the dish and discard the marinade. Braai the chicken, skin side down first, over **direct medium heat**, with the lid closed, until the meat is firm to the touch and opaque all the way to the centre, 8–12 minutes, turning once or twice and brushing generously with the reserved reduced marinade during the last few minutes of braaiing time. (Check within the first few minutes to make sure the skin does not burn.) Remove from the braai and leave to rest for 3–5 minutes. Place one chicken breast on each plate. Spoon the remaining ¼ cup reduced marinade equally over top. Add the coriander to the salsa and serve alongside.

SERVES: 4

THAI-MARINATED CHICKEN
WITH SPICY DIPPING SAUCE

PREP TIME: 25 minutes
MARINATING TIME: 2 to 8 hours
BRAAIING TIME: 45 to 50 minutes
LEVEL OF SPICINESS: 6/10

Sauce
½ cup hot water
4 teaspoons sugar
2 tablespoons fresh lime juice
2 tablespoons fish sauce
1 small red Thai chilli, thinly sliced, with seeds
1 teaspoon crushed garlic

Marinade
1 stalk lemongrass, bulbous bottom part only, outer
    layers peeled, coarsely chopped
¼ cup Thai fish sauce
¼ cup packed light brown sugar
2 tablespoons coarsely chopped fresh coriander
    leaves and tender stems
4 garlic cloves, coarsely chopped
2 small red Thai chillies, thinly sliced, with seeds

1 whole chicken, cut into 8 serving pieces,
    or a full braai-pack

Glaze
¼ cup honey
2 teaspoons hot chilli-garlic sauce, such as Sriracha

1. In a small bowl, whisk the hot water and the sugar to dissolve the sugar. Stir in the remaining sauce ingredients. Cover and refrigerate while the chicken marinates.

2. In a food processor, purée the marinade ingredients (small bits should still be visible). Place the chicken pieces in a large, resealable plastic bag and pour in the marinade. Press the air out of the bag and seal tightly. Massage the marinade into the skin, and refrigerate for 2–8 hours.

3. Prepare the braai for indirect and direct cooking over medium-high heat 200°–260°C (400°–500°F).

4. In a small bowl, whisk the glaze ingredients; set aside at room temperature.

5. Brush the cooking grates clean. Braai the chicken pieces, skin side down first, over ***indirect medium-high heat***, with the lid closed as much as possible, until the juices run clear and the meat is no longer pink at the bone, 45–50 minutes, turning once or twice. During the last 5 minutes of braaiing time, brush the chicken all over with the honey mixture, and then slide over direct heat to crisp the skin, turning occasionally. Remove from the braai and leave to rest for about 5 minutes. Using a cleaver or a heavy knife, cut the thighs across in half and the breasts across into thirds. Pour the dipping sauce into small bowls, and serve right away.

SERVES: 6

SPICY JAMBALAYA

PREP TIME: 40 minutes
BRAAIING TIME: 16 to 20 minutes
LEVEL OF SPICINESS: 8/10

350 grams smoked sausages, such as Spanish
    chorizo, andouille or Polish kielbasa
3 firm, ripe tomatoes

Rub
1 teaspoon paprika
1 teaspoon coarse sea salt
½ teaspoon ground cayenne pepper

4 large boneless, skinless chicken thighs
Extra-virgin olive oil
1 medium onion, finely chopped (about 1 cup)
1 green and 1 red pepper, cut into 1.5-cm dice
2 garlic cloves, crushed
1½ cups uncooked long-grain white rice
2 teaspoons paprika
1 teaspoon dried thyme
1 teaspoon coarse sea salt
½ teaspoon ground cayenne pepper
½ teaspoon ground black pepper
2¾ cups chicken stock
1 bay leaf
1 teaspoon Tabasco sauce
½ cup roughly chopped fresh Italian parsley leaves

1. Prepare the braai for direct cooking over medium heat 180°–230°C (350°–450°F).

2. Brush the cooking grates clean. Braai the sausages and tomatoes over *direct medium heat*, with the lid closed, until the sausages are golden brown and the tomatoes are blackened and blistered all over, turning occasionally. The sausages will take 6–8 minutes, the tomatoes 8–10 minutes. Place the tomatoes in a bowl, cover with cling wrap to trap the steam and leave for 5–10 minutes. Peel away and discard the charred skin, then core and coarsely chop them. Cut the sausages into 1.5-cm slices.

3. Combine the rub ingredients. Brush the chicken thighs on both sides with oil and season evenly with the rub. Braai over *direct medium heat*, with the lid closed, until the meat is firm and the juices run clear, 8–10 minutes, turning once or twice. Transfer to a cutting board. Cut into 2-cm pieces.

4. In a large saucepan over medium heat, warm 2 tablespoons oil. Add the onion and peppers and sauté until softened, about 4 minutes, stirring occasionally. Add the garlic and sauté until fragrant, about 1 minute. Add the rice, paprika, thyme, salt, cayenne pepper and black pepper; stir to combine. Add the chicken stock, bay leaf and chopped tomatoes. Bring to a boil, then reduce the heat to a very low simmer. Cover and cook until the rice is fully cooked, 20–30 minutes. Stir in the chicken, sausage and Tabasco. Cover and cook over low heat until warmed throughout, 3–5 minutes. Remove the bay leaf and garnish with the parsley. Serve warm.

SERVES: 4

TANGERINE CHICKEN

PREP TIME: 25 minutes
MARINATING TIME: 6 to 8 hours
BRAAIING TIME: 30 to 50 minutes
LEVEL OF SPICINESS: 3/10

1 whole chicken, or a full braai-pack
6 tangerines (satsuma, naartjie), about 1.2 kg total
¼ cup plus 1 tablespoon soy sauce
¼ cup vegetable oil
2 tablespoons fresh lemon juice
1 tablespoon plus ¼ teaspoon peeled, crushed fresh
    ginger, divided
½ teaspoon ground black pepper
2 tablespoons finely chopped fresh coriander leaves

1. Cut the whole chicken into eight pieces: two thighs, two drumsticks, two wings with some breast meat attached (remove and discard the wing tips), and two smaller breast pieces. Place in a deep baking dish just large enough to hold the pieces in one layer.

2. Finely grate the zest from two of the tangerines and transfer to a blender. Cut away the peel and white pith of these tangerines and dice their flesh. Cover and refrigerate the diced tangerines until ready to serve. Juice three of the remaining tangerines directly into the blender. Roughly chop the final tangerine – peel, pith and all – and add it to the blender.

3. To the contents of the blender add the soy sauce, oil, lemon juice, 1 tablespoon of the ginger, and the pepper. Blend until almost smooth, 10–15 seconds. Pour the marinade over the chicken, massaging it into the meat and under the skin. Cover and refrigerate for 6–8 hours, turning occasionally.

4. Prepare the braai for indirect cooking over medium heat 180°–230°C (350°–450°F).

5. Remove the chicken from the dish and reserve the marinade. Pour the reserved marinade into a small saucepan and bring to a boil over medium-high heat. Boil for 2 full minutes, whisking occasionally. Set by the braai.

6. Brush the cooking grates clean. Braai the chicken pieces, skin side up first, over *indirect medium heat*, with the lid closed, until the juices run clear and the meat is no longer pink at the bone. The wings and breasts will take 30–40 minutes and the thighs and drumsticks will take 40–50 minutes. Begin turning and basting with the boiled marinade after 25 minutes of braaiing time. If desired, to brown and crisp the skin, move the chicken pieces over direct heat during the last 5 minutes, turning once or twice. Remove from the braai and rest for 3–5 minutes.

7. In a small bowl combine the refrigerated, diced tangerines with the coriander and the remaining ¼ teaspoon ginger. Serve right away with the chicken. Serving suggestion: Charred Corn Salad (for recipe, see page 127).

SERVES: 4

BASQUE CHICKEN HALVES
WITH PEPPERS, SMOKED HAM AND OLIVES

PREP TIME: 30 minutes
MARINATING TIME: 4 to 10 hours
BRAAIING TIME: about 1 hour
SPECIAL EQUIPMENT: instant-read thermometer
LEVEL OF SPICINESS: 6/10

Marinade

1 tablespoon smoked paprika
1 tablespoon sherry wine vinegar
1 tablespoon finely chopped fresh thyme leaves
3 garlic cloves, finely chopped
1½ teaspoons coarse sea salt
¾ teaspoon ground black pepper
¾ teaspoon crushed red chilli flakes

Extra-virgin olive oil
1 whole chicken, 1.5–2 kg, halved lengthways,
    backbone, giblets and any excess fat removed

Dressing

2 tablespoons sherry wine vinegar
2 teaspoons smoked paprika
1 teaspoon coarse sea salt
½ teaspoon ground black pepper
¼ teaspoon crushed red chilli flakes

2 large peppers, 1 red and 1 green, cut into 4 planks
1 large onion, cut across into 0.5-cm slices
1 gammon steak, about 180 grams and 0.5 cm thick
½ cup kalamata olives, each cut in half
⅓ cup roughly chopped fresh Italian parsley leaves

1. In a shallow baking dish, whisk the marinade ingredients, including ¼ cup oil. Place the chicken in the dish and turn to coat. Cover and refrigerate for 4–10 hours, turning the chicken occasionally.

2. Prepare the braai for direct and indirect cooking over medium heat 180°–230°C (350°–450°F).

3. Combine the dressing ingredients. Then slowly whisk in ¼ cup oil until the dressing is emulsified. Brush the peppers and the onion with oil.

4. Brush the cooking grates clean. Remove the chicken from the dish and discard the marinade. Braai the chicken, bone side down first, over **indirect medium heat**, with the lid closed, until the juices run clear and an instant-read thermometer inserted into the thickest part of the thigh (not touching the bone) registers 70°–75°C, 45–55 minutes, turning once or twice. Remove from the braai and leave to rest for 10–15 minutes (the internal temperature will rise 5–10 degrees during this time). Braai the peppers, the onion and gammon steak over **direct medium heat**, with the lid closed, until the vegetables are tender and grill marks appear on the gammon, turning once or twice. The vegetables will take 8–10 minutes and the gammon about 5 minutes. Cut the vegetables and the gammon into 2-cm dice.

5. To the dressing add the diced vegetables and gammon, the olives and the parsley; toss to coat. Divide the mixture among four to six plates. Cut each chicken half into two or three pieces and add a piece of chicken to each plate. Serve immediately.

SERVES: 4 to 6

BEER CAN CHICKEN
GLAZED WITH MOLASSES AND HOT MUSTARD

PREP TIME: 30 minutes
BRAAIING TIME: 1¼ to 1½ hours
SPECIAL EQUIPMENT: punch-style can opener;
large disposable foil tray; 2 handfuls hickory
or oak wood chips, soaked in water for at least
30 minutes; instant-read thermometer
LEVEL OF SPICINESS: 5/10

Rub
2 tablespoons paprika
2 teaspoons coarse sea salt
2 teaspoons packed light brown sugar
1 teaspoon ground cayenne pepper
1 teaspoon mustard powder
½ teaspoon garlic powder
½ teaspoon onion powder
½ teaspoon ground black pepper

1 whole chicken, 1.8–2 kg, neck, giblets and any
    excess fat removed
2 teaspoons canola oil
1 can beer

Glaze
2 tablespoons mustard powder
2 tablespoons cider vinegar
½ cup molasses
2 tablespoons spicy brown mustard
½ teaspoon coarse sea salt
½ teaspoon ground black pepper

1. In a small bowl, mix the rub ingredients.

2. Brush the chicken with the oil and season all over, including inside the cavity and under the legs and wings, with the rub, pressing firmly to adhere. Fold the wing tips behind the chicken's back.

3. Open the can of beer and pour out about two-thirds (or add it to the soaking wood chips). Using a punch-style can opener, make two more holes in the top of the can. Place the can on a solid surface, then lower the chicken cavity over the can.

4. Place a large disposable foil tray underneath the cooking grates (over an unlit burner) to catch the drippings. Prepare the braai for indirect cooking over medium heat 180°–230°C (350°–450°F).

5. In a small bowl, whisk the mustard powder and the vinegar. Leave to stand for 5 minutes. Whisk in the remaining glaze ingredients.

6. Brush the cooking grates clean. Drain and add the wood chips to the charcoal or to the smoker box of a gas braai, following manufacturer's instructions. When the wood begins to smoke, transfer the chicken-on-a-can to the braai, balancing it on its two legs and the can like a tripod. Cook the chicken over *indirect medium heat*, centred over the foil tray, with the lid closed, until the skin is brown and crisp, the juices run clear, and an instant-read thermometer inserted into the thickest part of the thigh (not touching the bone) registers 70°–75°C,

about 1¼–1½ hours. Keep the temperature of the braai between 180° and 200°C (350°–400°F). If using a charcoal braai, replenish the charcoal as needed to maintain a steady temperature, adding 6–10 unlit briquettes after 45 minutes. Leave the lid off the braai for about 5 minutes to help the new briquettes light. During the last 15 minutes of cooking time, gently dab half of the glaze over the chicken (try to avoid brushing off the rub).

7. Carefully remove the chicken-on-a-can from the braai (do not spill the contents of the beer can, which will be very hot), and coat it again with some of the glaze. Leave the chicken to rest for 5–10 minutes (the internal temperature will rise by 5–10 degrees during this time) before lifting it from the can and carving into serving pieces. Serve the chicken warm with the remaining glaze as a sauce.
Serving suggestion: Spicy Maple Baked Beans (for recipe, see page 132).

SERVES: 4

CHICKEN FRA DIAVOLO

PREP TIME: 20 minutes
MARINATING TIME: 3 to 4 hours
BRAAIING TIME: 40 minutes to 1 hour
SPECIAL EQUIPMENT: large cast-iron frying pan
or 2 foil-wrapped bricks, poultry shears,
instant-read thermometer
LEVEL OF SPICINESS: 5/10

Marinade

¼ cup extra-virgin olive oil
1 tablespoon finely grated lemon zest
3 garlic cloves, crushed
2 teaspoons paprika
2 teaspoons coarse sea salt
1 teaspoon dried origanum
1 teaspoon crushed red chilli flakes
1 teaspoon ground black pepper
1 teaspoon ground cayenne pepper

1 whole chicken, 1.8–2 kg, neck, giblets, and any
    excess fat removed

1. In a small bowl, whisk the marinade ingredients.

2. Place the chicken, breast side down, on a cutting
board. Using poultry shears, cut from the neck to the
tail end, along either side of the backbone and remove
the backbone. Once the backbone is out, you'll be able
to see the interior of the chicken. Make a small slit in
the cartilage at the end of the breastbone. Then,
placing both hands on the rib cage, crack the chicken
open like a book. Run your fingers along either side
of the cartilage in between the breasts to loosen it
from the flesh. Grab the bone and pull up on it, to
remove the bone along with the attached cartilage.
The chicken should now lie flat. Pat dry.

3. Place the chicken in a shallow baking dish. Rub
the marinade all over the chicken. Loosen the skin
under the breasts and thighs, if desired, and rub
some marinade underneath the skin. Cover with
cling wrap and refrigerate for 3–4 hours.

4. Prepare the braai for direct and indirect cooking
over medium-low heat 150°–200°C (300°–400°F).

5. Brush the cooking grates clean. Place the chicken,
skin side down, over *direct medium-low heat*, and put
a large cast-iron pan, or two foil-wrapped bricks,
directly on top. Close the lid and braai until the skin
is browned, 10–15 minutes, but watch carefully that
the skin does not burn. Wearing insulated barbecue
mitts, remove the pan and, using a large spatula, turn
the chicken over. Slide the chicken over *indirect
medium-low heat*, replace the pan, and continue
braaiing, with the lid closed, until the juices run clear
and an instant-read thermometer inserted into the
thickest part of the thigh (not touching the bone)
registers 70°–75°C, 30–45 minutes more. Remove
from the braai and leave to rest for 10–15 minutes
(the internal temperature will rise by 5–10 degrees
during this time).

6. Cut the chicken into serving pieces and
serve warm.

SERVES: 4 to 6

CHICKEN CHILAQUILES

PREP TIME: 20 minutes
BRAAIING TIME: 21 to 28 minutes
SPECIAL EQUIPMENT: large, heavy (3-litre minimum capacity) flame-proof pan (do not use cast iron)
LEVEL OF SPICINESS: 7/10

1 tablespoon prepared chilli powder
1½ teaspoons coarse sea salt
⅛ teaspoon ground cayenne pepper
6 large boneless, skinless chicken thighs
Extra-virgin olive oil
1 medium onion, finely chopped
2 teaspoons crushed garlic
1 can (410 grams) crushed tomatoes
1 cup chicken stock
3 canned chipotle chilli peppers in adobo sauce,
    finely chopped
200 grams coarsely crushed tortilla chips, divided
1 cup fresh or frozen (unthawed) corn kernels
½ cup crumbled feta cheese
2 tablespoons coarsely chopped fresh coriander

NOTE!

Chilaquiles (chee-LA-kee-lays) is a one-dish Mexican casserole of tortilla chips cooked with a spicy sauce. In this version, a tomato-chipotle sauce meets up with chicken and corn, but you could make a vegetarian version with flame-grilled courgettes and black beans, or even scrambled eggs.

1. In a small bowl, combine the chilli powder, salt and cayenne pepper. Brush the chicken thighs on both sides with oil and season evenly with the spices. Leave the chicken to stand at room temperature for 15–30 minutes before braaiing.

2. Prepare the braai for direct and indirect cooking over medium heat 180°–230°C (350°– 450°F).

3. Meanwhile, in a large, heavy, flame-proof pan over medium heat, warm 2 tablespoons oil. Add the onion and garlic and cook until softened, about 3 minutes, stirring occasionally. Add the tomatoes, stock and chopped chipotle chillies and bring to a boil. Reduce the heat to medium-low and simmer until slightly reduced, about 5 minutes, stirring often. Remove from the heat. Add half the tortilla chips, allowing them to soften.

4. Brush the cooking grates clean. Braai the chicken over *direct medium heat*, with the lid closed as much as possible, 6–8 minutes, turning once or twice (the chicken will finish cooking in the sauce). Remove from the braai and cut into bite-sized pieces.

5. Scatter the chicken and corn on top of the sauce. Add the remaining tortilla chips, spooning the sauce over the chips. Place the pan on the braai over *indirect medium heat* and cook, with the lid closed, until the sauce is simmering, 15–20 minutes. Turn off the burners, but leave the pan on the cooking grates. Top the chilaquiles with the feta and leave to stand for 5 minutes. Garnish with coriander and serve warm.

SERVES: 6

SPICED DUCK BREASTS
WITH CHIPOTLE CHERRY SALSA

PREP TIME: 30 minutes
BRAAIING TIME: about 8 minutes
LEVEL OF SPICINESS: 5/10

Salsa

2 cups fresh cherries, pitted *or* frozen pitted cherries,
    thawed and drained
½ cup coarsely chopped red onion
½ cup tightly packed fresh coriander leaves and
    tender stems
1 canned chipotle chilli pepper in adobo sauce
Juice of 1 large lime
¾ teaspoon coarse sea salt
½ teaspoon sugar
1 small clove garlic, thinly sliced
¼ teaspoon ground black pepper

Rub

2 tablespoons paprika
1 tablespoon packed light brown sugar
2 teaspoons coarse sea salt
1½ teaspoons dried origanum
1 teaspoon chipotle chilli powder
½ teaspoon ground cumin
½ teaspoon ground cinnamon
½ teaspoon ground black pepper

4 deboned duck breast halves (with skin),
    each 180–200 grams, patted dry
2 tablespoons roughly chopped fresh coriander leaves

1. In a food processor, combine the salsa ingredients. Using short pulses, process the ingredients just until they are finely chopped but not puréed. Taste and add more lime juice, salt or sugar, if desired.

2. Prepare the braai for direct cooking over medium heat 180°–230°C (350°–450°F).

3. In a small bowl, combine the rub ingredients.

4. Slip your fingers beneath the skin and fat on the duck breasts to loosen it from the meat. Using kitchen shears or a sharp knife, trim away some of the skin and fat, leaving a 2.5-cm-wide strip that runs the entire length of each breast. Score the skin and fat three to four times on the diagonal (do not cut through the meat). This trimming and slashing procedure will help prevent flare-ups and will allow the fat to melt and the skin to crisp during braaiing. Season evenly with the rub.

5. Brush the cooking grates clean. Braai the duck, skin side down first, over ***direct medium heat***, with the lid closed as much as possible, until cooked to your desired doneness, about 8 minutes for medium rare, turning once (if flare-ups occur, move the duck temporarily over indirect heat). Transfer to a cutting board and leave to rest for 5 minutes.

6. Cut the duck breasts on the diagonal into 1-cm-thick slices. Fan the slices out on serving plates and drizzle with any accumulated juices. Spoon the salsa alongside or over the top, garnish with chopped coriander, and serve right away.

SERVES: 4 to 6

CHIPOTLE TURKEY BURGERS
WITH PICKLED ONIONS

PREP TIME: 20 minutes
MARINATING TIME: 30 minutes to 1 hour
BRAAIING TIME: 10 to 12 minutes
LEVEL OF SPICINESS: 5/10

Onions

1 medium red onion, very thinly sliced
¼ cup fresh lime juice
¼ cup fresh orange juice
1 teaspoon sugar
½ teaspoon coarse sea salt

Patties

900 grams minced turkey, preferably dark meat
½ cup finely chopped onion
½ cup finely chopped fresh coriander leaves
2 canned chipotle chilli peppers in adobo sauce,
    finely chopped
1 small Thai (bird's-eye) chilli, seeded and chopped
2 teaspoons coarse sea salt
2 garlic cloves, crushed
1 teaspoon chipotle chilli powder
½ teaspoon ground cumin
½ teaspoon ground black pepper

6 hamburger buns, split
1 ripe avocado, cut into 0.5-cm slices

1. In a medium bowl, combine the onion ingredients. Cover and marinate at room temperature for between 30 minutes and 1 hour.

2. In a large bowl, gently combine the patty ingredients. With wet hands, form the mixture into six patties of equal size, each about 2 cm thick. Don't compact the meat too much or the patties will be tough. With your thumb or the back of a spoon, make a shallow indentation about 2.5 cm wide in the centre of each patty. This will help the patties cook evenly and prevent them from puffing on the braai. Refrigerate the patties until ready to braai.

3. Prepare the braai for direct cooking over medium heat 180°–230°C (350°–450°F).

4. Brush the cooking grates clean. Braai the patties over **direct medium heat**, with the lid closed as much as possible, until fully cooked but still juicy, 10–12 minutes, turning once when the patties release easily from the grate without sticking (if flare-ups occur, move the patties temporarily over indirect heat). During the last minute of braaiing time, toast the buns, cut side down, over direct heat.

5. Serve the patties hot on the toasted buns, topped with the pickled onions and avocado slices. Serving suggestion: Coleslaw with Jalapeño, Coriander and Lime (for recipe, see page 126).

SERVES: 6

TURKEY ESCALOPES
WITH WASABI BROWN BUTTER AND MIZUNA

PREP TIME: 15 minutes, plus about
20 minutes for the butter
BRAAIING TIME: 2 to 3 minutes
LEVEL OF SPICINESS: 7/10

2 tablespoons wasabi powder
2 tablespoons warm water
½ cup (125 grams) unsalted butter
4 teaspoons prepared horseradish
2 teaspoons rice vinegar or cider vinegar
1 teaspoon coarse sea salt, divided
¾ teaspoon ground black pepper, divided
1 deboned, skinless turkey breast, about 700 grams
2 tablespoons toasted sesame oil
2½ tablespoons sesame seeds
450 grams mizuna (mustard greens), tough stems
    trimmed, leaves coarsely chopped
1 tablespoon crushed garlic
1 tablespoon peeled, crushed fresh ginger
½ teaspoon crushed red chilli flakes
1 tablespoon soy sauce

1. In a small saucepan, combine the wasabi powder and the water and leave to stand for 10 minutes.

2. In a large, deep pan over medium-low heat, melt the butter until the liquid turns golden and the solids brown on the bottom of the pan, 8–10 minutes, swirling the pan occasionally. Remove from the heat and cool slightly. Whisk the brown butter and transfer all but 1 tablespoon to the saucepan with the wasabi mixture. Add the horseradish, vinegar, ¼ teaspoon salt and ¼ teaspoon pepper to the wasabi mixture and whisk until smooth.

3. Prepare the braai for direct cooking over medium-high heat 200°–260°C (400°–500°F).

4. Cut the turkey breast across into four equal portions. One at a time, place each portion between two sheets of cling wrap and pound to a 15–20 cm diameter and an even 5 mm thickness.

Place each slice of turkey breast between two sheets of cling wrap and pound with a small, heavy pan. Hit the meat first in the centre, then push the pan towards the thinner edges at the perimeter. Eventually you should have an even thickness of about 5 mm from edge to edge.

You should be left with four thin escalopes of meat. Brush each escalope on both sides with the oil and season evenly with the remaining ¾ teaspoon salt, ½ teaspoon pepper, and the sesame seeds.

5. Brush the cooking grates clean. Braai the escalopes over *direct medium-high heat*, with the lid closed as much as possible, until the meat is firm to the touch and no longer pink in the centre, 2–3 minutes, turning once. Transfer the meat to warm plates and cover with foil to keep warm.

6. Return the pan with the reserved brown butter over medium heat. When hot, add the mizuna, garlic, ginger and chilli flakes. Cover and cook for 1 minute, then rotate the mizuna from top to bottom and cook, uncovered, until the mizuna just begins to wilt, about 1 minute more. Remove from the heat and stir in the soy sauce.

7. Briefly reheat and whisk the wasabi brown butter in the saucepan, then pour it over the turkey and top with the wilted mizuna. Serve right away.

SERVES: 4

PRAWN TAILS
WITH BLOODY MARY COCKTAIL SAUCE

PREP TIME: 30 minutes
MARINATING TIME: 30 minutes
BRAAIING TIME: 2 to 4 minutes
LEVEL OF SPICINESS: 6/10

Marinade

3 tablespoons extra-virgin olive oil
3 tablespoons fresh lemon juice
2 teaspoons paprika
1 teaspoon Tabasco sauce
1 teaspoon coarse sea salt
1 teaspoon ground black pepper

1 kg king prawn tails, peeled and deveined

Sauce

½ cup fresh lemon juice
½ cup tomato sauce
2 tablespoons tomato paste
2 tablespoons minced canned chipotle chilli peppers
    in adobo sauce
2 tablespoons vodka (optional)
1 tablespoon Worcestershire sauce
2 teaspoons white prepared horseradish
¼ teaspoon coarse sea salt

2 limes, cut into wedges

1. In a small bowl, whisk the marinade ingredients. Place the prawn tails in a large, resealable plastic bag, and pour in the marinade. Press the air out of the bag and seal tightly. Turn the bag to distribute the marinade, place the bag in a bowl and refrigerate for 30 minutes.

2. Prepare the braai for direct cooking over high heat 230°–290°C (450°–550°F).

3. In a medium bowl, whisk the sauce ingredients.

4. Brush the cooking grates clean. Remove the prawns from the bag and discard the marinade. Braai the prawns over *direct high heat*, with the lid closed as much as possible, until they are firm to the touch and just turning opaque in the centre, 2–4 minutes, turning once or twice. Serve the prawns warm with the sauce and the lime wedges.

SERVES: 4 to 6 as an appetizer

SPICY PRAWN TOSTADAS

WITH ROASTED VEGETABLE SALSA

PREP TIME: 30 minutes
BRAAIING TIME: 14 to 20 minutes
LEVEL OF SPICINESS: 5/10

1 small onion, cut crossways into 1.5-cm slices
Extra-virgin olive oil
4 ripe tomatoes, halved lengthways
1 medium red pepper, cut into 4 planks
500 grams king prawn tails, peeled and deveined
1½ teaspoons prepared chilli powder
Coarse sea salt
⅛ teaspoon ground cayenne pepper

Chipotle cream
½ cup sour cream
1 canned chipotle chilli pepper in adobo sauce,
    finely chopped
1 teaspoon adobo sauce (from the can)

¼ cup coarsely chopped fresh coriander leaves
2 tablespoons fresh lime juice
2 canned chipotle chilli peppers in adobo sauce,
    finely chopped
1 tablespoon finely chopped jalapeño chilli, seeded
    or with seeds
1 teaspoon crushed garlic
6 flour tortillas (20 cm)
1 ripe avocado, diced

1. Prepare the braai for direct cooking over
medium-high heat 200°–260°C (400°–500°F).

2. Brush the cooking grates clean. Brush the onion
slices with oil. Braai the onion, tomatoes and red
pepper over *direct medium-high heat*, with the lid
closed, until the onion is tender and the tomato and
pepper are blackened and blistered, 8–12 minutes,
turning occasionally. Remove from the braai. Place
the pepper in a bowl and cover with cling wrap to trap
the steam; set aside for at least 10 minutes.

3. Coat the prawns with 1 tablespoon oil and season
with the chilli powder, ¼ teaspoon salt and the cayenne
pepper. Brush the cooking grates clean. Braai the
prawns over *direct medium-high heat*, with the lid
closed, until they are firm to the touch and just opaque
in the centre, 4–6 minutes, turning once. Remove
from the braai, cool, and cut in half lengthways.

4. Lower the braai's temperature to medium heat
180°–230°C (350°–450°F) and prepare the braai
for direct and indirect cooking. Combine the
chipotle cream ingredients. Slip the tomatoes from
their skins. Remove and discard the pepper skins. In
a food processor, pulse the onion, tomatoes, pepper,
coriander, lime juice, chipotle chillies, jalapeño and
garlic until finely chopped. Season with salt.

5. Warm the tortillas over *direct medium heat*, with
the lid open, for about 1 minute. Flip, grilled side
up, and slide over indirect heat. Spread each tortilla
evenly with the salsa and scatter the prawns and
diced avocado on top. Slide over *direct medium heat*,
and braai until the undersides are lightly toasted,
30 seconds to 1 minute more. Remove from the braai.
Drizzle with the chipotle cream and serve warm.

SERVES: 4 to 6

LEMONGRASS PRAWNS
IN LETTUCE LEAVES

PREP TIME: 30 minutes
BRAAIING TIME: 7 to 11 minutes
SPECIAL EQUIPMENT: cast-iron pan or wok
LEVEL OF SPICINESS: 5/10

700–800 grams king prawn tails, peeled, deveined
    and roughly chopped
3 tablespoons vegetable oil, divided
½ teaspoon ground black pepper
2 large lemongrass stalks
1 piece fresh ginger, about 2.5 cm long, peeled
    and roughly chopped
3 large garlic cloves, peeled
2 tablespoons packed light brown sugar
4 teaspoons Thai red curry paste
3 tablespoons fresh lime juice
2 tablespoons fish sauce
2 teaspoons cornflour (Maizena), dissolved
    in 1 tablespoon water
1 cup diced, unpeeled English cucumber
1 cup cherry tomatoes, each cut in half
⅓ cup roughly chopped fresh coriander leaves
¼ cup thinly sliced fresh basil leaves
8 large butter lettuce leaves

1. In a bowl, toss the prawns with 1 tablespoon of the oil and the black pepper.

2. If necessary, cut off the bottom 10 cm of each lemongrass stalk and reserve; discarding the tops. Peel off and discard the tough outer layers of the bottom end of the stalks (about three to four layers) until only the inner, tender white parts remain.

Roughly chop the inner stalks and put them in a food processor. Add the ginger and the garlic and blend until finely chopped. Transfer to a bowl.

3. Prepare the braai for direct cooking over high heat 230°–290°C (450°–550°F).

4. In one bowl, combine the brown sugar and curry paste. In a second bowl, combine the lime juice and fish sauce. Bring these bowls, the prawns, the lemongrass mixture, the cornflour mixture and the remaining 2 tablespoons oil to the braai.

5. Place a cast-iron pan over *direct high heat*, add the remaining 2 tablespoons oil and close the lid until the oil is hot, about 1 minute. Add the lemongrass mixture and stir-fry, with the lid open, until the mixture softens slightly, 1–2 minutes (do not brown). Stir in the brown sugar-curry paste, followed by the lime juice-fish sauce mixture. Cook, with the lid closed, until the liquid is slightly thickened and reduced, 1–2 minutes. Add the prawn tails and stir to blend. Cook, with the lid closed, until the prawns are firm to the touch and just turning opaque in the centre, 3–5 minutes more (juices will form from the prawns). Add the cornflour mixture and boil just until the juices thicken slightly, about 30 seconds, stirring constantly.

6. Wearing insulated barbecue gloves, carefully transfer the pan to a heatproof surface. Stir in the cucumber, tomatoes, coriander and basil. Arrange two lettuce leaves on each plate. Spoon the prawn mixture on top and serve right away.

SERVES: 4

BRAAIED SCALLOPS
WITH CHILLI DIPPING SAUCE

PREP TIME: 10 minutes, plus about
20 minutes for the sauce
BRAAIING TIME: 4 to 6 minutes
LEVEL OF SPICINESS: 3/10

Sauce
1 medium carrot, peeled and cut into 5 mm slices
    (about ½ cup)
1 cup water
2 teaspoons soy sauce
1 teaspoon hot chilli-garlic sauce, such as Sriracha
¼ teaspoon ground cumin
1 tablespoon rice vinegar
1 tablespoon extra-virgin olive oil
1 teaspoon finely chopped fresh mint leaves

20 jumbo sea scallops, each about 30–50 grams
Extra-virgin olive oil
Coarse sea salt
Ground black pepper

1. Place the carrot slices in a small saucepan along with the water, soy sauce, Sriracha and cumin. Bring the mixture to a boil. Lower the heat to a simmer and cook until the carrots are just tender, about 15 minutes. Transfer the mixture to a food processor and purée, adding the vinegar, oil and mint while the motor is running. The sauce should have the consistency of tomato sauce. If it seems too thick, add a bit more water. If it seems too thin, return it to the saucepan and simmer for a few more minutes to reduce.

2. Prepare the braai for direct cooking over high heat 230°–290°C (450°–550°F).

3. Rinse the scallops under cold running water and pat dry. Remove and discard the small, tough side muscle that might be left on each one. Place the scallops in a medium bowl, lightly coat with oil, and season evenly with salt and pepper.

4. Brush the cooking grates clean. Braai the scallops over **_direct high heat_**, with the lid closed as much as possible, until they are lightly browned and just opaque in the centre, 4–6 minutes, turning once. Remove from the braai and serve warm with the sauce drizzled on top or in small dipping bowls.

SERVES: 4

SMOKED BLACK MUSSELS
IN SPICY MARINARA OVER LINGUINE

PREP TIME: 20 minutes
BRAAIING TIME: about 10 to 15 minutes
SPECIAL EQUIPMENT: large disposable foil tray;
2 handfuls aromatic wood chips (such as oak or
apple), soaked in water for at least 30 minutes
LEVEL OF SPICINESS: 6/10

Marinara
¼ cup extra-virgin olive oil
1 small onion, finely chopped
3 green chillies, seeded and finely chopped
3 large garlic cloves, crushed
½ cup dry white wine
2 cans (400 grams each) Italian tomatoes in juice,
    undrained
2 canned chipotle chilli peppers in adobo sauce,
    finely chopped
1 tablespoon adobo sauce (from the can)
2 canned anchovy fillets, crushed or 1 teaspoon
    anchovy paste (optional)
½ teaspoon coarse sea salt
½ teaspoon ground black pepper

3 dozen whole black mussels, rinsed and scrubbed
340 grams dried linguine or spaghetti
3 tablespoons finely chopped fresh basil or
    Italian parsley

1. In a large pan over medium-high heat, warm
the oil. Add the onion, chillies and garlic and cook
until lightly browned, about 4 minutes, stirring
occasionally. Add the wine and bring to a boil. Add
the remaining marinara ingredients and return to a
boil. Reduce the heat to medium-low and cook for
about 10 minutes, stirring occasionally.

2. Prepare the braai for direct cooking over medium
heat 180°–230° C (350°– 450°F).

3. Bring a large pot of salted water to a boil. Pour
1 cup of the marinara sauce into a disposable foil
tray large enough to hold the mussels in a single layer.
Add the mussels. Drain and add the wood chips to
the charcoal or to the smoker box of a gas braai,
following manufacturer's instructions, and close the
lid. When the wood begins to smoke, set the tray of
mussels over **direct medium heat** and cook, with the
lid closed, until the mussels open, 10–15 minutes,
stirring occasionally. Discard any mussels that do
not open. Meanwhile, cook the linguine in the pot
of boiling water according to package instructions.

4. Drain the linguine and toss with the marinara
in the tray. Divide among plates and top with the
mussels. If desired, drizzle the remaining marinara
sauce from the foil tray over the mussels and linguine,
being careful to leave behind any sand that may have
emerged from the mussels during steaming.
Scatter the chopped basil or parsley over the top.
Serve immediately.

SERVES: 4

GRIDDLED LINEFISH ESCABÈCHE
WITH CITRUS AND CHILLIES

PREP TIME: 40 minutes
BRAAIING TIME: 4 to 6 minutes
MARINATING TIME: 6 hours to 2 days
SPECIAL EQUIPMENT: flameproof griddle pan,
rubber gloves
LEVEL OF SPICINESS: 8/10

Marinade

1 habanero chilli
3 tablespoons extra-virgin olive oil
1 large onion, quartered vertically and thinly sliced
3 garlic cloves, finely chopped
Finely grated zest and juice of 3 lemons, 3 oranges,
     and 3 limes
2 tablespoons red wine vinegar
½ teaspoon coarse sea salt
¼ teaspoon ground black pepper
2 tablespoons finely chopped fresh Italian parsley

4 fresh linefish fillets, each 180–200 grams and
     2 cm thick, skin removed
Extra-virgin olive oil
1 tablespoon chilli powder

NOTE!

Escabèche was brought to Spain by the Moors
where it became a popular way of preserving
fish; the highly acidic marinade serves as a
sort of pickle. Typically, fish is simply cooked
in the sauce, but in this recipe the fish is
briefly braaied, giving it a charred nuance that
complements the marinade's spiciness.

1. Prepare the braai for direct cooking over high heat 230°–290°C (450°–550°F) and place a flameproof griddle pan on the braai to preheat.

2. Wearing rubber gloves (to avoid burning your skin), remove and discard the stem and seeds from the habanero. Finely chop the habanero. In a large pan over medium-high heat, warm the oil. Add the onion and sauté until translucent, about 3 minutes. Add the habanero and the garlic and sauté for 1 minute more. Add the citrus zest and juice, the vinegar, salt and pepper; bring to a boil. Remove from the heat and stir in the parsley.

3. Generously brush both sides of the linefish fillets with oil and season evenly with the chilli powder. Place the fillets on the griddle pan and cook over ***direct high heat***, with the lid closed as much as possible, until the fish is barely cooked and still moist in the centre, 4–6 minutes, turning once. Transfer the fillets to a large, shallow, glass baking dish. Pour the marinade over the fillets and leave to cool to room temperature. Cover and refrigerate for at least 6 hours, or up to 2 days.

4. Remove the linefish fillets from the refrigerator about 1 hour before serving. Serve the fillets topped with some of the marinade.

SERVES: 4; 8 as an appetizer

SPICED YELLOWTAIL
WITH MANGO-AVOCADO SALSA

PREP TIME: 20 minutes
CHILLING TIME: 30 minutes
BRAAIING TIME: 4 to 5 minutes
SPECIAL EQUIPMENT: perforated grill pan
LEVEL OF SPICINESS: 7/10

Salsa

2 ripe mangoes, each about 300 grams, cut into
    1.5-cm dice
¼ cup finely diced red pepper
2 spring onions (white and light green parts only),
    thinly sliced on the bias
3 tablespoons coarsely chopped fresh coriander
1½ tablespoons fresh lime juice
1 tablespoon hot chilli-garlic sauce, such as Sriracha
½ teaspoon coarse sea salt
¼ teaspoon Tabasco sauce
1 small ripe avocado

Rub

2 teaspoons ground coriander
1½ teaspoons ground cumin
1 teaspoon chipotle or ancho chilli powder
1 teaspoon coarse sea salt
½ teaspoon ground black pepper
¼ teaspoon ground cayenne pepper

4 portions yellowtail, or firm-fleshed fish, each about
    200 grams and 2.5 cm thick, skin removed
Vegetable oil
2 teaspoons fresh lemon juice

1. In a bowl, combine the mango, red pepper, spring onions, coriander, lime juice, Sriracha, salt and Tabasco. Toss gently and refrigerate for about 30 minutes (but not longer than 1 hour, or the fruit will get mushy). Just before serving, dice and fold in the avocado.

2. In a small bowl, combine the rub ingredients. Generously brush both sides of each fish portion with oil and season evenly with the rub.

3. Prepare the braai for direct cooking over medium-high heat 200°–260°C (400°–500°F) and place a perforated grill pan on the braai to preheat.

4. Braai the fish portions on the grill pan over *direct medium-high heat*, with the lid closed as much as possible, until the flesh is opaque in the centre but still moist, 4–5 minutes, carefully turning once with a metal spatula after 3 minutes.

5. Transfer the fish to a serving platter and drizzle each portion with ½ teaspoon lemon juice. Mound the salsa on the side, and serve right away.

SERVES: 4

YELLOWTAIL

WITH JERK SEASONING AND PAPAYA SALAD

PREP TIME: 40 minutes
MARINATING TIME: 1 to 2 hours
BRAAIING TIME: 8 to 10 minutes
LEVEL OF SPICINESS: 6/10

Marinade

¼ cup plus 2 tablespoons extra-virgin olive oil
1 tablespoon peeled, crushed fresh ginger
3 garlic cloves, crushed
3 small Thai chillies, thinly sliced, with seeds
1 teaspoon ground allspice
½ teaspoon ground nutmeg
¼ teaspoon ground cinnamon
2 tablespoons packed light brown sugar
1½ tablespoons finely chopped fresh thyme leaves
3 spring onions, trimmed and thinly sliced
⅓ cup fresh lime juice

Coarse sea salt
Ground black pepper
4 yellowtail portions, each about 180 grams
     and 4 cm thick

Dressing

2 teaspoons finely grated lime zest
3 tablespoons fresh lime juice
2 tablespoons packed light brown sugar
1½ tablespoons extra-virgin olive oil

1 large, firm, ripe papaya, cut into 2-cm pieces
4 cups packed, roughly torn butter lettuce leaves
¾ cup loosely packed fresh coriander leaves
⅓ cup roughly chopped, roasted salted cashews

1. In a heavy based pan over medium-high heat, warm 2 tablespoons of olive oil. Add the ginger, garlic and chillies and stir for 1 minute. Add the allspice, nutmeg and cinnamon; stir until fragrant, then add the brown sugar and the thyme, stirring until the sugar melts, about 1 minute. Cool slightly. Transfer to a food processor. Add the spring onions, lime juice, 1 teaspoon salt, ¾ teaspoon pepper and the remaining ¼ cup oil and process until blended. Transfer ¼ cup of the marinade to a bowl and reserve, covered and refrigerated. Remove from the refrigerator 1 hour before serving.

2. Arrange the yellowtail in a glass dish, pour over the remaining marinade, and turn to coat. Cover and refrigerate for 1–2 hours, turning occasionally.

3. Prepare the braai for direct cooking over high heat 230°–290°C (450°–550°F).

4. Whisk the dressing ingredients, including ½ teaspoon salt and ½ teaspoon pepper. Put the papaya into a bowl and drizzle with 2 tablespoons of the dressing. In another bowl, combine the lettuce and the coriander.

5. Brush the cooking grates clean. Braai the fish over **direct high heat**, with the lid closed, until the flesh begins to flake when poked with the tip of a knife, 8–10 minutes, turning once. Transfer a portion to each of four plates. Spoon the reserved ¼ cup marinade over the fish. Toss the salad with the remaining dressing. Mound some salad on each plate, top with papaya and cashews and serve right away.

SERVES: 4

CUBAN-SPICED TUNA TACOS

PREP TIME: 30 minutes
MARINATING TIME: 1 hour
BRAAIING TIME: 8 to 10 minutes
LEVEL OF SPICINESS: 7/10

Marinade
1 large spring onion, finely chopped
¼ cup coarsely chopped fresh coriander leaves
3 tablespoons extra-virgin olive oil
3 tablespoons fresh lemon juice
2 teaspoons crushed garlic
1 teaspoon ground cumin
½ teaspoon coarse sea salt
½ teaspoon ground cayenne pepper

1 tuna steak, 250–300 grams and about 3 cm thick

Salsa
2 firm ripe tomatoes, seeded and cut into 0.5-cm dice
½ cup canned black beans, rinsed and drained
¼ cup finely chopped white onion, rinsed
    and drained
2 tablespoons finely chopped fresh coriander leaves
2 tablespoons finely chopped canned chipotle chilli
    pepper in adobo sauce
¾ teaspoon coarse sea salt
¼ teaspoon ground black pepper

4 flour tortillas (25 cm)
¼ head iceberg lettuce, shredded
1 firm, ripe avocado, diced
2 limes, quartered

1. In a nonreactive bowl, combine the marinade ingredients and transfer half of the marinade to a small baking dish. Place the tuna in the dish and rub the marinade into both sides of the fish with your fingers. Refrigerate, covered, for 1 hour. Reserve the remaining marinade.

2. Prepare the braai for direct and indirect cooking over medium-high heat 200°–260°C (400°–500°F).

3. In a medium bowl, combine the salsa ingredients. Wrap the tortillas in an aluminum foil packet.

4. Brush the cooking grates clean. Braai the tuna over *direct medium-high heat*, with the lid closed as much as possible, until just turning opaque throughout, 8–10 minutes, turning once. During the last 2 minutes of braaiing time, warm the tortilla packet over indirect heat, turning once. Transfer the tuna to a cutting board and cut into 3-cm cubes; toss quickly with the reserved marinade.

5. Serve the tuna warm in the tortillas with lettuce, salsa and avocado, squeezing lime juice over the top.

SERVES: 4

HAKE AND SWEET POTATOES
WITH MUSTARD-LEMON AÏOILI

PREP TIME: 30 minutes
BRAAIING TIME: 15 to 20 minutes
SPECIAL EQUIPMENT: cast-iron griddle pan
LEVEL OF SPICINESS: 6/10

Aïoli

½ cup mayonnaise
2 tablespoons French mustard
2 tablespoons finely chopped fresh basil leaves
2 tablespoons finely chopped fresh chives
1 teaspoon finely grated lemon zest
2 teaspoons fresh lemon juice
1 teaspoon Tabasco sauce

Extra-virgin olive oil
Coarse sea salt
Ground black pepper
500–600 grams sweet potatoes, peeled and
     sliced into 5 mm rings
1 cup flour
1 teaspoon bicarbonate of soda
1 can lager beer
1½ teaspoons Tabasco sauce
600 grams fresh hake or line fish fillets
     (4 × 150 gram portions)
1 lemon, cut into wedges

1. Prepare the braai for direct cooking over high heat 230°–290°C (450°–550°F) and place a griddle pan or ridged cast-iron pan on the braai to preheat.

2. In a small bowl, whisk the aïoli ingredients. Cover and refrigerate until serving time.

3. In another bowl, whisk 1 tablespoon oil with 1 teaspoon salt and ½ teaspoon pepper. Add the sweet potato slices and toss to coat.

4. In a large bowl, whisk the flour, 1½ teaspoons salt, 1 teaspoon pepper and the bicarbonate of soda. Add the beer and the Tabasco and whisk well. Place the fish in the bowl and gently coat with the batter.

5. Pour 3 tablespoons oil onto the griddle. When the oil is hot, spread the potatoes in a single layer on the griddle and cook over **direct high heat**, with the lid closed, until they are golden brown and tender, 7–8 minutes, turning once or twice and adjusting the heat if the potatoes are browning too quickly. Transfer the potatoes to a warm platter. Using a slotted spoon, place half the fish pieces on the hot griddle and braai, with the lid closed, until the fish is a golden on the outside and the flesh is opaque but still moist, 4–6 minutes, turning once. Add more oil to the griddle as needed. Repeat with the remaining fish. During the last minute of braaiing time, braai the lemon wedges on the cooking grates over direct heat, turning once.

6. Divide the potato slices and the fish among four plates. Spoon the aïoli alongside each serving and serve warm with the braaied lemon wedges.

SERVES: 4

SMOKED TANDOORI SALMON
WITH TARRAGON-MUSTARD SAUCE

PREP TIME: 30 minutes
MARINATING TIME: 4 to 6 hours
BRAAIING TIME: 6 to 10 minutes
SPECIAL EQUIPMENT: 1 handful hickory wood
chips, soaked in water for at least 30 minutes
LEVEL OF SPICINESS: 6/10

Paste

1 tablespoon paprika
2 teaspoons ground coriander
2 teaspoons ground cumin
2 teaspoons garam masala
1 teaspoon ground ginger
1 teaspoon turmeric
½ teaspoon ground cayenne pepper
¾ cup plain Greek yoghurt
3 tablespoons fresh lemon juice
2 tablespoons vegetable oil
4 garlic cloves, crushed
1 teaspoon coarse sea salt
½ teaspoon ground black pepper

4 salmon fillets (with skin), each 180–200 grams
      and about 2.5 cm thick, pin bones removed

Sauce

½ cup dry white wine
⅓ cup finely chopped shallots
1 tablespoon yellow mustard seeds
¾ cup heavy whipping cream
2 tablespoons finely chopped fresh tarragon leaves
1 tablespoon spicy brown (French) mustard
¼ teaspoon coarse sea salt
¼ teaspoon ground black pepper

Vegetable oil

1. In a frying pan over medium heat, combine the paprika, coriander, cumin, garam masala, ginger, turmeric and cayenne pepper, and cook until fragrant and slightly darker, 1–2 minutes, stirring occasionally. Transfer to a bowl and stir in the remaining paste ingredients. Reserve 2 tablespoons of the paste; cover and refrigerate until needed. Place the salmon fillets in a glass dish. Spread the remaining paste over both sides of the fillets. Cover and refrigerate for 4–6 hours.

2. In a saucepan over high heat, combine the wine, shallots and mustard seeds. Boil until all but about 3 tablespoons of the liquid has cooked away, 2–4 minutes. Add the cream and boil gently until the sauce thickens slightly, 1–2 minutes more. Remove from the heat and whisk in the tarragon, mustard, salt and pepper. Stir in 1 tablespoon of the reserved paste. Taste and add more reserved paste by the teaspoonful if desired. Reheat before serving.

3. Prepare the braai for direct cooking over high heat 230°–290°C (450°–550°F).

4. Brush the cooking grates clean. Brush the fillets with oil. Drain and add the wood chips to the charcoal or to the smoker box of a gas braai, following manufacturer's instructions, and close the lid. When the wood begins to smoke, cook the fillets, flesh side down first, over **direct high heat**, with the lid closed, until cooked to medium rare, 6–10 minutes, turning once after 5–7 minutes. Slip a spatula between the skin and flesh and, leaving the skin behind, transfer the fillets to serving plates. Spoon the sauce on top.

SERVES: 4

BRAAIED SALMON
WITH SMOKY TOMATO-CHIPOTLE SAUCE

PREP TIME: 20 minutes, plus about
45 minutes for the sauce
BRAAIING TIME: 8 to 11 minutes
SPECIAL EQUIPMENT: 3/10

Sauce
2 tablespoons extra-virgin olive oil
½ cup finely chopped red onion
2 teaspoons crushed garlic
1 teaspoon dried origanum
2 cans (400 grams each) whole tomatoes in juice
1 canned chipotle chilli pepper in adobo sauce
½ teaspoon sugar
½ teaspoon coarse sea salt
¼ teaspoon ground black pepper

4 salmon fillets (with skin), each 180–200 grams
    and about 2.5 cm thick, pin bones removed
Extra-virgin olive oil
Coarse sea salt
Ground black pepper

1. In a medium saucepan over medium-high heat, warm the oil. Add the onion and cook until soft, 4–5 minutes, stirring occasionally. Stir in the garlic and origanum and cook until the garlic is light brown, about 1 minute more. Add the remaining sauce ingredients and bring to a boil. Reduce the heat to low and simmer for 30–40 minutes, stirring occasionally and crushing the tomatoes with the back of a large spoon as they soften. Carefully pour the sauce into the bowl of a food processor or a blender. Purée and return to the pan. Keep the sauce warm over low heat.

2. Prepare the braai for direct cooking over high heat 230°–290°C (450°–550°F).

3. Generously brush both sides of each fillet with oil and season evenly with salt and pepper. Brush the cooking grates clean. Braai the fillets, flesh side down first, over *direct high heat*, with the lid closed as much as possible, until you can lift the fillets off the cooking grates without sticking, 6–8 minutes. Turn the fillets over and continue to cook to your desired doneness, 2–3 minutes more for medium rare. Slip a spatula between the skin and the flesh and, leaving the skin behind, transfer the fillets to serving plates. Serve warm with the sauce.
Serving suggestion: Stuffed Courgettes (for recipe, see page 123).

SERVES: 4

BRAAIED POTATO SALAD
WITH SMOKED TROUT, RED ONION AND SPICY GREENS

PREP TIME: 15 minutes
BRAAIING TIME: about 15 minutes
SPECIAL EQUIPMENT: perforated grill pan
LEVEL OF SPICINESS: 7/10

500–600 grams baby potatoes, scrubbed
        but not peeled, halved lengthways
1½ tablespoons extra-virgin olive oil
½ teaspoon coarse sea salt
½ teaspoon ground cayenne pepper
¼ teaspoon ground black pepper

Vinaigrette
¼ cup plus 2 tablespoons extra-virgin olive oil
2 tablespoons red or white wine vinegar
2 tablespoons Dijon mustard
2 teaspoons prepared horseradish
½ teaspoon coarse sea salt
¼ teaspoon ground cayenne pepper

1 medium red onion, cut across into 1.5-cm slices
Extra-virgin olive oil
Coarse sea salt
Ground black pepper
5 cups loosely packed wild rocket
300 grams smoked trout fillets, flaked with a fork

1. Prepare the braai for direct cooking over medium heat 180°–230°C (350°–450°F). Place a perforated grill pan on the braai to preheat.

2. Place the potatoes in a medium bowl and toss thoroughly with the oil, salt, cayenne pepper and black pepper.

3. In a large bowl, whisk the vinaigrette ingredients until smooth.

4. Brush the cooking grates clean. Lightly brush the onion slices on both sides with oil and season evenly with salt and pepper. Spread the potatoes and the onion slices in a single layer on the grill pan and cook over *direct medium heat*, with the lid closed as much as possible, until lightly browned and tender, about 15 minutes, turning occasionally. Transfer to a cutting board and leave to rest for about 5 minutes. Roughly chop the onions and the potatoes.

5. Add the chopped onions, potatoes and the rocket to the bowl with the vinaigrette and fold together gently to coat all the ingredients. Divide the salad evenly among plates, scattering the flaked trout over the top. Serve immediately.

SERVES: 4 to 6

TIP!
You can braai almost any kind of potato over direct heat by first cutting it into pieces about one centimetre thick. This will allow the pieces to cook all the way to the centre before the outsides turn too dark.

SWEET AND SPICY NUTS

PREP TIME: 10 minutes
COOLING TIME: about 1 hour
BRAAIING TIME: about 1 hour
SPECIAL EQUIPMENT: 2 large disposable foil trays
LEVEL OF SPICINESS: 7/10

Sweet nut crunch
1 cup raw pumpkin seeds (*pepitas*)
1 cup whole raw almonds
2 tablespoons unsalted butter, melted
1 tablespoon honey
1 tablespoon packed brown sugar
1 teaspoon ground cinnamon
1 teaspoon coarse sea salt
½ teaspoon ground cayenne pepper
¼ teaspoon ground nutmeg

Spicy nuts
1 cup raw pumpkin seeds (*pepitas*)
1 cup whole raw almonds
1 cup roasted red-skin peanuts
2 teaspoons hot chilli oil
1 teaspoon extra-virgin olive oil
1 teaspoon coarse sea salt
1 teaspoon paprika
1 teaspoon Worcestershire sauce
½ teaspoon ground cayenne pepper

1. Prepare the braai for indirect cooking over low heat 160°–180°C (250°–350°F).

2. To make the sweet nut crunch, spread the pumpkin seeds and the almonds evenly in a large disposable foil tray. Braai over **indirect low heat**, with the lid closed as much as possible, until the nuts are fragrant and lightly toasted, about 15 minutes, stirring occasionally. Remove the tray from the braai.

3. In a small bowl, combine the remaining sweet nut crunch ingredients. Drizzle the mixture over the toasted nuts and toss to coat evenly. Return the pan over **indirect low heat**, close the lid, and cook for 20–25 minutes more, stirring occasionally. Remove from the braai. Leave the nuts to cool in the pan for 1 hour. Break into bite-sized pieces.

4. To make the spicy nuts, spread the pumpkin seeds and almonds in a large disposable foil tray. Braai over **indirect low heat**, with the lid closed as much as possible, until the nuts are fragrant and lightly toasted, about 15 minutes, stirring occasionally. Remove the tray from the braai and add the peanuts.

5. In a small bowl, whisk the remaining spicy nut ingredients. Drizzle the mixture over the nuts and toss to coat evenly. Return the pan over **indirect low heat**, close the lid, and cook for 5–7 minutes more, stirring once or twice. Remove from the braai and spoon the nuts onto paper towels. Leave to cool.

6. Serve the nut mixtures in separate bowls. If not serving immediately, store in airtight containers.

SERVES: 20 as an appetizer

SMOKY BRINJAL 'CAVIAR'

PREP TIME: 10 minutes
STANDING TIME: 30 minutes to overnight
BRAAIING TIME: about 1 hour
LEVEL OF SPICINESS: 4/10

2 brinjals, about 1 kg total
1 large egg
1 large garlic clove, crushed
1 small Thai chilli, seeded and finely chopped
Coarse sea salt
½ teaspoon white wine vinegar
¼ teaspoon ground black pepper
Extra-virgin olive oil
1 tablespoon finely chopped fresh coriander, mint
     or parsley leaves
Lemon wedges
5 pita breads, each cut into 8 wedges

1. Prepare the braai for direct and indirect cooking over medium heat 180°–230°C (350°–450°F).

2. Braai the whole brinjals over **direct medium heat**, with the lid closed as much as possible, until slightly charred in places, about 10 minutes, turning occasionally. Transfer to indirect heat and continue braaiing, with the lid closed, until the brinjals are very tender and the centres have collapsed, 50–60 minutes longer, turning over every 15–20 minutes. If the skin has naturally split, transfer split-side down to a colander set over a large bowl (or the sink) and leave to drain for at least 30 minutes or up to 2 hours. (Or, place in the refrigerator, cover with a kitchen towel and drain overnight.) If the skin has not naturally split on the braai, slit it with a knife, then proceed as previously directed. You want the flesh to weep and drain.

3. Pull off and discard the brinjal's skin (don't worry if you can't get it all, the little black bits add a nice, smoky flavour). Squeeze the brinjals gently to extract a little more of the water. Cut the brinjal flesh into rough chunks, removing any large seed sacs.

4. Place the egg (still in the shell) in a mug and cover with boiling water. Leave to stand for exactly 1 minute to coddle.

5. In a food processor, combine the brinjal, garlic, chilli, ¾ teaspoon salt, the vinegar and the pepper. Crack in the coddled egg. Purée until very smooth, scraping down the sides of the bowl as necessary. With the motor running, add ⅔ cup oil very slowly, processing until the mixture is a smooth, fluffy paste. (Some food processors have a small hole for this purpose in the 'pusher'. Pour in the oil and watch it drip slowly through.)

6. Transfer to a serving bowl and stir in the coriander. Cover and refrigerate for 1 hour to allow the flavours to blend. (The dip will keep in the refrigerator for up to 1 day.) Leave to stand for 30 minutes to come to room temperature. Season with salt, squeeze a lemon wedge over top and drizzle with 1 teaspoon oil. Serve with the pita wedges.

SERVES: 6 to 8

VEGETABLE MUFFULETTA

PREP TIME: 45 minutes
BRAAIING TIME: about 8 minutes
CHILLING TIME: 1 to 3 hours
LEVEL OF SPICINESS: 8/10

Relish

1 cup roughly chopped brine-cured black olives
2 tablespoons green peppercorns in brine,
    drained and chopped
1 tablespoon crushed garlic
2 teaspoons red wine vinegar
1 teaspoon crushed red chilli flakes
1 teaspoon ground cayenne pepper
½ teaspoon dried thyme or marjoram

Extra-virgin olive oil
Ground black pepper
Coarse sea salt
1 medium white onion, cut across into 1-cm slices
2 large courgettes, cut lengthways into 0.5-cm slices
3 brinjals, each cut lengthways into 1-cm slices
2 large red peppers, each cut into 4 planks
1 baguette or ciabatta loaf, 8–10-cm wide and
    about 30 cm long
½ cup ready-made basil pesto
1 cup tightly packed wild rocket
120 grams thinly sliced provolone cheese

1. Prepare the braai for direct cooking over medium heat 180°–230°C (350°–450°F).

2. In a large bowl, combine the relish ingredients, including 2 tablespoons oil, 1 teaspoon black pepper, and ½ teaspoon salt.

3. Lightly brush the onion, courgettes and brinjal slices and red pepper planks with oil and season with salt and pepper.

4. Brush the cooking grates clean. Braai the vegetables over **direct medium heat**, with the lid closed, until they are charred in spots and very tender, turning once or twice. The courgettes will take about 4 minutes, the red pepper 6–8 minutes, and the onion and brinjal about 8 minutes. Put the onion, courgettes and brinjal slices into the bowl with the relish; toss to coat. Put the red pepper planks into a small bowl and cover with cling wrap to trap the steam. Leave to stand for 5–10 minutes, then peel away and discard the skin. Then add them to the bowl with the rest of the vegetables; toss to coat.

At first the layers will stack high above the bread, but after you put the 'lid' in place and weight the sandwich, everything will be compacted, with no air pockets, so it will be easy to slice.

5. Cut off the top one-third of the loaf horizontally. Scoop out most of the soft bread from inside the bottom section, leaving a 1.5-cm outer crust. Scoop out some bread from the top section of the loaf in the same way.

6. Spread the pesto evenly over the inside of the top and bottom of the loaf. Arrange half the vegetables and half the relish on the bottom section, starting with the onions and distributing the vegetables evenly. Press down firmly to compact the vegetables; there should be no air pockets. Top with a layer of rocket, then provolone, pressing down firmly.

Finish with the remaining vegetables and the remaining relish, laying them parallel to the loaf and mounding them up higher than the top opening. Replace the top of the loaf, press down firmly and wrap tightly in several layers of cling wrap. Place the muffuletta on a baking sheet, place another baking sheet on top, and weight the top with something heavy, such as several large cans. Chill for at least 1 hour or up to 3 hours. Unwrap and, using a serrated knife, cut the muffuletta into six equal portions. Serve right away.

SERVES: 6

BEETROOT AND APPLE SALAD
WITH HORSERADISH DRESSING

PREP TIME: 25 minutes
BRAAIING TIME: 1 to 2 hours, depending
on the size of the beetroot
LEVEL OF SPICINESS: 5/10

4 medium beetroots, about 500 grams total
Extra-virgin olive oil

Dressing
2 medium shallots, finely chopped
¼ cup extra-virgin olive oil
2 tablespoons fresh lemon juice
2 teaspoons finely grated lemon zest
2 teaspoons prepared horseradish
2 teaspoons spicy brown mustard
1 teaspoon ground black pepper
¾ teaspoon green peppercorns in brine, drained
½ teaspoon coarse sea salt

2 Granny Smith apples, peeled and cut into
    bite-sized pieces
100 grams loose-leaf lettuce, cut into bite-sized pieces
⅔ cup coarsely grated Pecorino-Romano or
    Parmesan-style cheese, divided
60 grams roughly chopped walnuts

1. Prepare the braai for indirect cooking over
medium heat 180°–230°C (350°–450°F).

2. Trim off any leafy tops and root ends from the
beetroots and scrub them under cold water. Lightly
brush them all over with oil. Brush the cooking
grates clean. Braai the beetroots over **indirect
medium heat**, with the lid closed as much as possible,
until they are tender when pierced with the tip of a
knife, 1–2 hours, depending on their size, turning
occasionally. Transfer the beetroots to a bowl, cover
with cling wrap, and leave to stand until cool enough
to handle, about 25 minutes. With a sharp paring
knife, peel away and discard the skins. Cut the
beetroots into bite-sized pieces and reserve.

3. In a large bowl, whisk the dressing ingredients
until smooth. Add the apples, lettuce and half the
cheese. Toss until thoroughly combined. Divide
the salad evenly among four plates and top with the
beetroots, the remaining cheese and the walnuts.
Serve immediately.

SERVES: 4

POTATO FLAPJACKS
WITH HORSERADISH APPLE SAUCE AND WATERCRESS SALAD

PREP TIME: 1 hour
BRAAIING TIME: 15 to 20 minutes
SPECIAL EQUIPMENT: large heatproof griddle
LEVEL OF SPICINESS: 3/10

Apple sauce
700 grams Granny Smith apples, peeled and cut
    into 2-cm pieces
1 cup apple juice
¼ cup sugar
⅛ teaspoon ground black pepper
2 tablespoons prepared horseradish, or to taste

Dressing
3 tablespoons extra-virgin olive oil
1 tablespoon white wine vinegar
1 teaspoon Dijon mustard
½ teaspoon coarse sea salt
½ teaspoon ground black pepper

1 large bunch watercress, trimmed
1 bunch radishes, trimmed and thinly sliced
1 large egg
1½ cups finely chopped onions, divided
1 teaspoon coarse sea salt
½ teaspoon ground black pepper
700 grams potatoes, peeled and cut into
    2.5-cm pieces
3 tablespoons cake flour
¼ cup vegetable oil or canola oil

1. In a saucepan, combine the apples, juice, sugar and pepper. Bring to a boil over high heat, stirring until the sugar dissolves. Reduce the heat to medium and simmer, uncovered, until the apples are very tender, 10–12 minutes, stirring occasionally. Remove from the heat and cool for 5 minutes. Transfer the mixture to a food processor and purée until almost smooth but some small pieces still remain. Transfer to a bowl, and leave to stand for about 15 minutes. Stir in the horseradish, and refrigerate until serving time.

2. Whisk the dressing ingredients. Set aside. In a bowl, combine the watercress and the radishes. Cover and refrigerate until serving time.

3. Prepare the braai for direct cooking over medium heat 180°–230°C (350°–450°F) and place a large heatproof griddle on the braai to preheat.

4. Whisk the egg. Mix in 1 cup of the onions, the salt and the pepper. In a food processor, combine the potatoes and the remaining ½ cup onions. Process until the potatoes are finely chopped and some of the mixture is puréed. Line a colander with a clean dish towel. Transfer the potato mixture to the towel-lined colander, wrap the towel tightly around the potatoes and squeeze out as much liquid as possible. Scrape the potato mixture into the bowl with the egg mixture. Add the flour, and mix with a fork.

5. Coat the griddle with the oil and, working in batches, ladle ¼ cup of the potato mixture onto the griddle, flattening each flapjack gently with the back of a spoon. Cook over **direct medium heat**, with the lid closed, until the flapjacks are browned on both sides, 8–12 minutes per flapjack, turning several times. Serve with the apple sauce and the salad.

SERVES: 4 to 6 (makes about 14 flapjacks)

BRAAIED CORN CHOWDER
WITH ROASTED TOMATOES AND CHILLIES

PREP TIME: 30 minutes
BRAAIING TIME: 10 to 12 minutes
LEVEL OF SPICINESS: 8/10

4 slices baguette, each about 1.5 cm thick
Extra-virgin olive oil
3 ripe, red tomatoes
3 green Thai chillies
4 fresh sweetcorn cobs, husks removed
1 medium onion, finely chopped (about 1 cup)
2 garlic cloves, crushed
1 teaspoon chipotle chilli powder
Coarse sea salt
½ teaspoon paprika
2–3 cups chicken stock
½ cup heavy whipping cream
¼ cup roughly chopped fresh coriander or basil leaves

1. Prepare the braai for direct cooking over medium heat 180°–230°C (350°–450°F).

2. Brush each baguette slice on both sides with oil. Brush the cooking grates clean. Braai the tomatoes, chillies and sweetcorn over *direct medium heat*, with the lid closed as much as possible, until the tomatoes and chillies are blackened and blistered all over and the corn is lightly charred, turning occasionally. The tomatoes and chillies will take 8–10 minutes, and the corn will take 10–12 minutes. During the last minute of braaiing time, toast the baguette slices, turning once. Remove from the braai as they are done.

3. Put the tomatoes and the chillies in a bowl and cover with cling wrap to trap the steam. Transfer the sweetcorn cobs to a cutting board. Leave the tomatoes and chillies to stand for about 10 minutes. Cut the kernels off the cobs. Reserve 1 cup of the kernels to add to the chowder after it has been puréed. Remove the tomatoes and chillies from the bowl and peel away and discard their charred skins. Core the tomatoes. Cut off and discard the chillies' tops and seeds. Coarsely chop the tomatoes and the chillies.

4. In a large pot over medium heat, warm 1 tablespoon oil. Add the onion and sauté until it begins to soften, about 3 minutes. Add the garlic and sauté until fragrant, about 1 minute. Add the chopped tomatoes and chillies, the sweetcorn, chilli powder, 1 teaspoon salt and the paprika. Sauté for about 2 minutes. Add 2 cups of the chicken stock (there should be enough stock to cover the vegetables; add more, if necessary). Bring to a boil, then reduce the heat to medium-low and simmer for about 5 minutes. Carefully transfer the mixture to a food processor or a blender and purée for 1 minute. With the motor running, add the cream in a steady stream. Return the chowder to the pot, stir in the reserved corn kernels and season with salt, if desired. If the chowder is too thick, thin with additional stock to your desired consistency. Bring to a simmer over medium-low heat to warm through.

5. Ladle the chowder into individual bowls, top with the coriander and serve warm with a baguette slice.

SERVES: 4

STUFFED RED PEPPERS
WITH JALAPEÑO PESTO

PREP TIME: 20 minutes
BRAAIING TIME: about 1 hour
SPECIAL EQUIPMENT: large disposable foil tray
LEVEL OF SPICINESS: 3/10

Stuffing
2 cups cooked long-grain rice (warm or at room
    temperature)
1 can (400 grams) black beans, rinsed and drained
120 grams feta or chevin (goat's cheese), crumbled
1 ripe tomato, finely diced
1 jalapeño chilli, seeded and finely chopped
2 spring onions (white and light green parts only),
    finely chopped
1 teaspoon dried origanum
1 teaspoon crushed garlic
½ teaspoon ground cumin

Coarse sea salt
Ground black pepper
3 large red peppers, halved lengthways, ribs and
    seeds removed

Pesto
1 jalapeño chilli, seeded and coarsely chopped
2 tablespoons toasted pumpkin seeds (*pepitas*)
    or pistachios
1 medium garlic clove, crushed
1 cup tightly packed fresh coriander leaves and
    tender stems
⅓ cup freshly grated Pecorino-Romano cheese
½ cup extra-virgin olive oil
1 teaspoon fresh lemon or lime juice

1. Prepare the braai for indirect cooking over
medium heat 180°–230°C (350°–450°F).

2. In a medium bowl, combine the stuffing
ingredients. Season with salt and pepper. Pack each
red pepper half with the stuffing, mounding it above
the rim. Arrange the peppers, stuffed sides up, in a
large disposable foil tray. Cover tightly with foil.

3. Braai the stuffed peppers in the tray over **indirect
medium heat**, with the lid closed, for 45 minutes.
Remove the foil covering and continue cooking, with
the lid closed, until the peppers are tender and the
stuffing is lightly browned, about 15 minutes more.
Meanwhile, prepare the pesto.

4. In a food processor or blender, pulse the jalapeño,
pumpkin seeds and garlic until finely chopped. Add
the coriander and the cheese and pulse until coarsely
chopped. With the motor running, gradually pour
the oil through the feed tube to make a thick paste.
Transfer the pesto to a small bowl. Add the lemon
juice and season with salt and pepper. Cover and
leave to stand at room temperature until the peppers
come off the braai.

5. Serve the stuffed peppers warm, topped with a
spoonful of pesto.

TIP!
You'll find jalapeño in the pesto and the
rice stuffing for a double dose of spiciness;
however, jalapeños vary a lot in their heat,
so your final level of spiciness may vary.

SUMMER VEGETABLE PASTA
WITH SPICY RICOTTA

PREP TIME: 20 minutes
BRAAIING TIME: 8 to 10 minutes
LEVEL OF SPICINESS: 6/10

1½ cups (375 grams) ricotta cheese
2 teaspoons crushed red chilli flakes, divided

Sauce
1 medium brinjal, cut across into 1.5-cm slices
1 medium onion, cut across into 1.5-cm slices
3 tablespoons extra-virgin olive oil
Coarse sea salt
3 ripe tomatoes
2 teaspoons crushed garlic

500 grams penne or any tubular pasta
¾ cup coarsely chopped fresh basil leaves, divided
½ cup freshly grated Parmigiano-Reggiano or
    Parmesan-style cheese
½ cup pitted briny black olives, coarsely chopped

1. Prepare the braai for direct cooking over medium heat 180°–230°C (350°–450°F).

2. Bring a large pot of salted water to a boil.

3. In a small bowl, mix the ricotta and 1 teaspoon of the chilli flakes. Leave to stand at room temperature while preparing the pasta and the sauce.

4. Brush the cooking grates clean. Brush the brinjal and onion slices on both sides with the oil and season with salt. Braai the brinjal, onion and tomatoes over **direct medium heat**, with the lid closed as much as possible, until the brinjal and onion are tender and the tomato skins split and are beginning to char, 8–10 minutes, turning once or twice. Remove from the braai. When cool enough to handle, slip the tomatoes from their skins. Roughly chop all the vegetables. In a food processor, combine the chopped vegetables with the garlic and remaining teaspoon of chilli flakes; pulse until coarsely chopped. Season with salt.

5. Cook the pasta in the boiling water until al dente, according to package instructions. Scoop out and reserve 1½ cups of the pasta water. Drain the pasta.

6. In the now-empty pasta pot, combine the sauce with ½ cup of the basil. Add the pasta, the pasta water, the cheese and the olives to the pot, and stir to combine. Divide the pasta evenly among six bowls. Top each with a large spoonful of the spicy ricotta and sprinkle evenly with the remaining ¼ cup basil. Serve right away.

SERVES: 6

COURGETTE FRITTERS
WITH HERBED LEMON CRÉME FRAÎCHE

PREP TIME: 40 to 45 minutes
DRAINING TIME: 30 minutes
BRAAIING TIME: 6 to 10 minutes per batch
SPECIAL EQUIPMENT: large heatproof griddle
LEVEL OF SPICINESS: 5/10

Crème fraîche
½ cup crème fraîche
1 tablespoon finely chopped fresh dill
1 tablespoon chopped fresh chives
1 teaspoon finely grated lemon zest
1 teaspoon fresh lemon juice
⅛ teaspoon coarse sea salt
⅛ teaspoon ground black pepper

Courgette fritters
500 grams large courgettes, trimmed and cut across
    into 8-cm pieces
1¼ teaspoons coarse sea salt, divided
8 large spring onions, ends trimmed,
    finely chopped (¾ cup)
¼ cup finely chopped fresh dill
¼ cup finely chopped fresh coriander leaves
¼ cup cake flour
1 large egg plus 1 egg white, beaten
2 tablespoons finely chopped jalapeño chilli,
    with seeds
1½ teaspoons curry powder
1 tcaspoon ground coriander
¼ teaspoon ground black pepper
½ cup crumbled feta cheese

Vegetable oil
Small fresh dill sprigs (optional)

1. Combine the crème fraîche ingredients. Cover and refrigerate while preparing the courgette fritters.

2. Using a food processor fitted with a grating disc with large or medium holes, grate the courgettes. (Alternately grate the courgettes on the large holes of a box grater.) Transfer the grated courgettes to a colander or strainer set over a bowl, sprinkle with 1 teaspoon of the salt, and toss to combine. Leave to stand for 30 minutes to allow excess moisture to drain. Working in batches, wrap the courgettes in a clean kitchen towel or several layers of paper towel and squeeze them as dry as possible. Scrape the courgettes into a bowl. Add the remaining fritter ingredients, including the remaining ¼ teaspoon salt. Stir gently with a fork and fold in the feta last.

3. Prepare the braai for direct cooking over medium heat 180°–230°C (350°–450°F) and place a large heatproof griddle on the braai to preheat.

4. Brush the cooking grates clean. Coat the griddle with 3 tablespoons oil and close the lid until the oil is hot, 2–3 minutes. Working in batches, drop the fritter mixture onto the griddle (2 tablespoons for small fritters or ¼ cup for larger fritters), flattening each fritter gently with the back of a spoon. Cook over ***direct medium heat***, with the lid closed, until deep golden on the bottom, 6–10 minutes (depending on their size), turning once. Remove from the braai. To serve, place two or three fritters on each plate, top each with a dollop of crème fraîche and garnish with dill sprigs.

SERVES: 4 to 6 as an appetizer (makes about 10 medium or 16 small fritters)

BLACK BEAN BURGERS
WITH CHIPOTLE SOUR CREAM

PREP TIME: 40 minutes
CHILLING TIME: 30 minutes
BRAAIING TIME: 6 to 8 minutes
SPECIAL EQUIPMENT: perforated grill pan
LEVEL OF SPICINESS: 8/10

⅓ cup sour cream
3 tablespoons finely chopped canned chipotle chilli
    peppers in adobo sauce, divided
1 tablespoon adobo sauce (from the can)
1 tablespoon finely chopped fresh coriander leaves
½ teaspoon Tabasco sauce

Patties
1 medium potato, about 240 grams
Vegetable oil
¼ cup finely chopped onion
2 stalks celery, finely chopped
2 tablespoons dry white wine
1½ teaspoons ground cumin
1½ teaspoons smoked paprika
1 teaspoon dried origanum
Ground black pepper
Coarse sea salt
1 tablespoon crushed garlic
1 can (400 grams) black beans, rinsed and drained
1 large egg, lightly beaten
¼ cup dried breadcrumbs
3 tablespoons finely chopped fresh coriander leaves

4 hamburger buns, split
4 radishes, cut into matchsticks

1. In a small bowl, whisk the sour cream with 1 tablespoon of the chopped chipotle chilli pepper, the adobo sauce, coriander and Tabasco. Refrigerate until serving time.

2. Peel the potato and cut into 1.5-cm cubes. In a saucepan of lightly salted boiling water, cook the potato cubes until completely tender but not falling apart, 6–8 minutes. Drain thoroughly in a colander.

3. In a large frying pan over medium heat, warm 2 tablespoons of oil. Sauté the onion and the celery in the oil until softened but not browned, about 5 minutes, stirring occasionally. Stir in the remaining 2 tablespoons chopped chipotle chilli pepper, the wine, cumin, paprika, origanum, 1 teaspoon pepper and 1 teaspoon salt; cook until the mixture is almost dry, about 2 minutes more. Reduce the heat to medium, stir in the garlic, beans and the potato cubes and cook to dry out the mixture thoroughly, 1–2 minutes more. Remove from the heat and leave to cool for 5–10 minutes.

4. Mash the mixture in the pan with a fork until all the potato pieces are fully mashed but the mixture is still chunky (a few of the beans will not be totally crushed). Work in the egg, breadcrumbs and coriander until evenly mixed. With wet hands, form the mixture into four compact patties of equal size, each about 8 cm in diameter and about 2.5 cm thick. Place the patties on a platter and refrigerate for 30 minutes.

5. Meanwhile, prepare the braai for direct cooking over medium-high heat 200°–260°C (400°–500°F); place a perforated grill pan on the braai to preheat.

6. Brush the cooking grates clean. Lightly brush both sides of each patty with oil and season with salt and pepper.

7. Place the patties on the grill pan and cook over **direct medium-high heat**, with the lid closed as much as possible, until browned and warm throughout, 6–8 minutes, turning once. During the last minute of braaiing time, toast the buns, cut side down, over direct heat. Remove the patties and buns from the braai, and build the burgers with a patty, a spoonful of chipotle sour cream, and a scattering of the radish matchsticks. Serve warm.

SERVES: 4

FALAFEL PATTIES
WITH TAHINI-GARLIC SAUCE

PREP TIME: 20 minutes
BRAAIING TIME: 6 to 8 minutes
LEVEL OF SPICINESS: 6/10

Sauce
½ cup well-stirred tahini
2–3 tablespoons fresh lemon juice
2 teaspoons crushed garlic
1 small red Thai chilli, finely chopped, with seeds
¾ cup hot water, as needed

Coarse sea salt

Patties
1 can (400 grams) chickpeas, rinsed, drained
    and patted dry
1 cup cold, cooked rice, preferably basmati
1 cup fresh breadcrumbs
¼ cup finely chopped red onion
1 large egg, beaten
2 tablespoons fresh lemon juice
2 tablespoons finely chopped fresh Italian parsley
    or coriander leaves
1 teaspoon ground cumin
1 small red Thai chilli, finely chopped, with seeds

Extra-virgin olive oil
2 ripe tomatoes, cored, seeded and diced
3 large Cos lettuce leaves, cut across into thin shreds
4 pita breads, tops cut off

1. In a medium bowl, whisk the tahini, lemon juice, garlic and chilli. Whisk in enough of the hot water to make a sauce with the consistency of thick heavy cream. Season with salt. Cover and set aside.

2. Prepare the braai for direct cooking over medium heat 180°–230°C (350°–450°F).

3. Line a baking sheet with waxed paper. In a food processor or a blender, combine the patty ingredients, including 1 teaspoon salt. Pulse for 10 one-second bursts to create a cohesive mass. Transfer to a medium bowl. With wet hands, gently form the mixture into four patties of equal size, about 10 cm in diameter. Place the patties on the lined baking sheet.

4. Brush the cooking grates clean. Lightly brush both sides of each patty with oil. Braai the patties over **direct medium heat**, with the lid closed as much as possible, until they are nicely browned, 6– 8 minutes, turning once. During the last minute of braaiing time, warm the pitas over direct heat, turning once.

5. Place a patty, tomatoes and lettuce inside each pita, and drizzle with the tahini sauce, as desired.

SERVES: 4

TIP!
Cold rice is best for this recipe, because it is stickier and will hold together better in patty form.

KOREAN BBQ TOFU
WITH SESAME SPINACH

PREP TIME: 30 minutes
FREEZING TIME: at least 4 hours
THAWING TIME: 1 hour to overnight
MARINATING TIME: 30 minutes to 1 hour
BRAAIING TIME: 8 to 12 minutes
LEVEL OF SPICINESS: 4/10

2 packs (350–450 grams each) extra-firm tofu,
    drained

Sauce

400 grams firm ripe pears, peeled, cored and
    roughly chopped
½ cup soy sauce
⅓ cup sake or dry sherry
4 spring onions, trimmmed and roughly chopped
2 tablespoons honey
1–2 Thai chillies, roughly chopped
1 tablespoon peeled, crushed fresh ginger
1 tablespoon toasted sesame oil
2 teaspoons rice vinegar
2 garlic cloves, roughly chopped

2 teaspoons vegetable oil
1 teaspoon toasted sesame oil
500 grams fresh baby spinach leaves
1 large spring onion (green part only), finely chopped
1 teaspoon toasted sesame seeds
¼ teaspoon crushed red chilli flakes

NOTE!

Freezing and thawing tofu ruptures the cells,
letting moisture flow out for a meatier texture
and allowing marinades to absorb more rapidly.

1. Cut each block of tofu across in half to make
two thick slabs (four slabs total). Wrap each slab
separately in cling wrap and freeze until solid, at
least 4 hours. Thaw the wrapped frozen tofu in the
refrigerator overnight or in a bowl of hot water,
replenishing the hot water as needed until the tofu
has thawed, 1–2 hours. Unwrap the tofu, wrap it in
clean kitchen towels, and place a flat weight on top
to squeeze out the excess water. Leave to stand for
30 minutes. Place the tofu in a shallow dish. In a food
processor, purée the sauce ingredients until relatively
smooth, about 1 minute, scraping down the sides
once. Pour 1 cup of the sauce over the tofu. Leave to
stand at room temperature for 30–60 minutes.

2. Prepare the braai for direct cooking over medium
heat 180°–230°C (350°–450°F).

3. In a large frying pan or wok over medium heat,
warm the vegetable and sesame oil. Add the spinach
by the handful and stir until just starting to wilt,
2–3 minutes. Remove from the heat. Add ½ cup of
the remaining sauce to the spinach and toss to coat.

4. Brush the cooking grates clean. Braai the tofu
over *direct medium heat*, with the lid closed, until
nicely browned, 8–12 minutes, turning once and
brushing with the sauce toward the end of braaiing
time to create a light glaze.

5. Cut each tofu slab into two triangles. Scatter the
spring onion over the tofu and serve the spinach
salad alongside, topped with sesame seeds and the
chilli flakes. Serve with the remaining sauce.

SERVES: 4

CHINESE GREEN BEANS

PREP TIME: 15 minutes
BRAAIING TIME: 8 to 11 minutes
SPECIAL EQUIPMENT: perforated grill pan,
large cast-iron frying pan
LEVEL OF SPICINESS: 9/10

500 grams fresh, tender green beans
2 tablespoons extra-virgin olive oil
Coarse sea salt

Sauce

¼ cup soy sauce
2 tablespoons unseasoned rice vinegar
1 tablespoon sugar
2–3 teaspoons hot chilli-garlic sauce, such as
    Sriracha
1 teaspoon Maizena (corn flour)
1 tablespoon extra-virgin olive oil
1 tablespoon peeled, finely chopped ginger
    with juices
2 garlic cloves, crushed
1 teaspoon crushed red chilli flakes

1. Prepare the braai for direct cooking over medium heat 180°–230°C (350°–450°F) and place a perforated grill pan on the braai to preheat.

2. Remove and discard the stem ends from the green beans. Place the beans in a bowl, pour in the oil and toss to coat evenly. Season with salt and toss again.

3. Using tongs, lift the green beans from the bowl and shake off any excess oil, letting it fall back into the bowl. Spread the beans on the grill pan in a single layer. Braai over **direct medium heat**, with the lid closed as much as possible, until the beans are browned in spots and crisp-tender, 5–7 minutes, turning occasionally. Transfer to a bowl.

4. In a small bowl, whisk the soy sauce, rice vinegar, sugar, Sriracha and Maizena.

5. Place a large cast-iron pan over **direct medium heat** to preheat. Add the oil, ginger, garlic and red chilli flakes to the pan and sauté until fragrant, about 2 minutes. Add the soy mixture, raise the heat to medium-high 200°–260°C (400°–500°F), and cook until slightly thickened, 1–2 minutes, stirring constantly. Add the green beans and turn to coat them with the sauce. Serve warm.

SERVES: 4

BRAAIED CHICORY WITH GINGER-HONEY DRESSING

PREP TIME: 15 minutes
BRAAIING TIME: 6 to 8 minutes
LEVEL OF SPICINESS: 6/10

½ lemon
4 heads chicory (endive, witloof), about
    500 grams total, each halved lengthways
Vegetable oil
Coarse sea salt
Ground black pepper

Dressing

3 tablespoons vegetable oil
2 tablespoons rice vinegar
2 tablespoons honey
1 teaspoon hot English mustard
1 teaspoon peeled, finely grated fresh ginger
1 teaspoon crushed garlic
¼ teaspoon ground cayenne pepper
¼ teaspoon ground white pepper

1 tablespoon finely chopped fresh chives
½–1 teaspoon crushed red chilli flakes

1. Add the lemon half to a medium pot of salted boiling water. Blanch the chicory in the water until barely softened, 1–2 minutes. Quickly drain and place the chicory in a bath of iced water to stop the cooking. When thoroughly cooled, remove from the water and pat dry with paper towels. Carefully trim away the tough triangular core from the base, leaving just enough so that the halves will hold together. Lightly brush the chicory all over with oil and season with salt and pepper.

2. Prepare the braai for direct cooking over medium-low heat 150°–200°C (300°–400°F).

3. In a small bowl, whisk the dressing ingredients until smooth.

4. Brush the cooking grates clean. Braai the chicory halves, cut side down, over ***direct medium-low heat***, with the lid closed as much as possible, until marked in places and tender, 6–8 minutes, turning once. Transfer to individual plates and spoon some of the dressing over the top. Scatter with the chives and the red chilli flakes. Serve immediately.

SERVES: 4

Side dishes

CHAR-GRILLED CORN WITH SPICY TOMATO BUTTER

PREP TIME: 5 minutes
BRAAIING TIME: 10 to 15 minutes
LEVEL OF SPICINESS: 5/10

Tomato Butter
¼ cup plus 2 tablespoons unsalted butter, softened
2 tablespoons tomato paste
1 chipotle chilli in adobo sauce (from a can), chopped
1 tablespoon Chinese-style chilli-garlic paste
¼ teaspoon garlic salt
¼ teaspoon coarse sea salt

6 fresh sweetcorn mealies, husks removed
Extra-virgin olive oil

1. Prepare the braai for direct cooking over medium heat 180°–230°C (350°–450°F).

2. In a small bowl, combine the butter ingredients.

3. Brush the cooking grates clean. Brush the corn all over with oil. Braai the sweetcorn over *direct medium heat*, with the lid closed, until the kernels are browned in spots and tender, 10–15 minutes, turning occasionally. Remove the from the braai.

4. Spread the sweetcorn with the tomato butter. Serve warm.

SERVES: 6

BRAISED RED CABBAGE WITH RED WINE AND BACON

PREP TIME: 20 minutes, plus about 1¼ hours to cook the cabbage
LEVEL OF SPICINESS: 1/10

3 slices thick-cut bacon, cut into 2.5-cm pieces
1 medium onion, finely chopped
2 Granny Smith apples, peeled, cored, and cut
  into 1.5-cm pieces
2 garlic cloves, finely chopped
½ cup full-bodied red wine
¼ cup red wine vinegar
1 kg red cabbage, thinly sliced
⅓ cup honey
1 bay leaf
¼ teaspoon ground cloves
1 teaspoon coarse sea salt
¾ teaspoon ground black pepper

1. In a large pot over medium-high heat, cook the bacon until crisp, 7–8 minutes, stirring occasionally. Using a slotted spoon, transfer the bacon to paper towels to drain. Add the onion to the bacon fat in the pot and cook until slightly softened, about 3 minutes, stirring occasionally. Add the apples and the garlic and stir until the garlic is fragrant, about 1 minute more.

2. In a small bowl, combine the wine and the vinegar. Gradually add the cabbage to the pot, pouring some of the wine mixture over each addition until all has been added. Add the honey, bay leaf and ground cloves and stir well.

3. Reduce the heat to medium-low and cover the pot tightly with a lid. Simmer until the cabbage is very tender, about 1¼ hours, stirring occasionally and adding a few tablespoons of water to the pot, as needed, if the liquid evaporates. During the last few minutes of cooking time, stir in the bacon and season with the salt and pepper. Discard the bay leaf. Serve hot.

SERVES: 6

TOMATO, CUCUMBER AND ONION SALAD

PREP TIME: 20 minutes
LEVEL OF SPICINESS: 1/10

Salad
3 large tomatoes, cored and cut into 1.5-cm slices
1 English cucumber, peeled and cut on the diagonal
    into thin slices
1 large red onion, cut across into thin slices
¼ cup torn fresh basil leaves
2 tablespoons torn fresh mint leaves
Coarse sea salt
Ground black pepper

Dressing
½ cup plain yoghurt
2 tablespoons extra-virgin olive oil
½ teaspoon crushed garlic

Whole fresh basil leaves (optional)
Black olives (optional)

1. On a large platter, arrange the tomato, cucumber and onion slices in overlapping circles. Scatter the basil and mint leaves on top, and season with salt and ground black pepper.

2. In a small bowl, whisk the dressing ingredients.

3. Drizzle the dressing over the salad. Garnish with the basil leaves and a few olives, if desired. Serve immediately.

SERVES: 4

WARM BEET AND ONION SALAD

PREP TIME: 30 minutes
BRAAIING TIME: 1 to 2 hours, depending on
the size of the beetroots
LEVEL OF SPICINESS: 1/10

2 medium golden beetroots with leafy tops,
    each about 6 cm in diameter
2 medium red beetroots with leafy tops,
    each about 6 cm in diameter
Extra-virgin olive oil

Dressing
1 medium orange
⅓ cup extra-virgin olive oil
2 tablespoons red wine vinegar
1 tablespoon finely sliced fresh basil leaves
1 teaspoon crushed garlic
½ teaspoon coarse sea salt
¼ teaspoon ground black pepper

1 large onion, cut across into 1.5-cm slices
Cos lettuce

1. Prepare the braai for indirect and direct cooking over medium heat 180°–230°C (350°– 450°F).

2. Trim the leafy tops from the beetroots leaving about 1.5 cm attached; reserve the tops. Leave the root ends intact, and scrub under cold water. Lightly brush with oil. Brush the cooking grates clean. Braai the beetroots over *indirect medium heat*, with the lid closed as much as possible,
until tender when pierced with the tip of a knife, 1– 2 hours, depending on their size, turning occasionally. Remove from the braai and leave to rest until cool enough to handle. Trim the ends from the beetroots and discard. Rub off the skins and cut into 1-cm slices. Place the red and golden beetroots in separate bowls (to keep the red beets from dying the golden beets red).

3. Wash and dry the orange. With a zester, scrape off 1 tablespoon of zest (or use a vegetable peeler to remove enough strips of zest to total 1 tablespoon when finely chopped). Reserve the zest. Cut the remaining skin and white pith from the orange and, working over a bowl, separate the orange into segments, letting the segments and any juice fall into the bowl. Add the reserved orange zest and the remaining dressing ingredients to the orange sections. Gently stir to combine.

4. Lightly brush the onion slices with some of the dressing and braai over *direct medium heat*, with the lid closed as much as possible, until tender, 10–12 minutes, turning once or twice. Remove from the braai and leave to cool slightly, then separate into rings.

5. Rinse the reserved leafy tops of the beetroots under cold water. Select the smallest, most tender leaves and place them with the lettuce in a large bowl. Add half the dressing and toss. Divide the lettuce mixture among four salad plates. Top with the beetroot slices and onion rings and drizzle over the remaining dressing. Serve warm or at room temperature.

SERVES: 4

VEGETABLE RATATOUILLE

PREP TIME: 25 minutes
BRAAIING TIME: 10 to 12 minutes
LEVEL OF SPICINESS: 1/10

1 medium onion, cut across into 1.5-cm slices
1 medium brinjal, cut lengthways into 1.5-cm slices
2–3 courgettes (baby marrows), cut lengthways into
    1.5-cm slices
2 small tomatoes, halved crossways, cored,
    and seeds removed
1 large red pepper, cut into quarters
Extra-virgin olive oil
Coarse sea salt
Ground black pepper
2 teaspoons crushed garlic
2 tablespoons finely chopped fresh basil leaves
2 teaspoons balsamic vinegar

1. Prepare the braai for direct cooking over medium heat 180°–230°C (350°–450°F).

2. Brush the cooking grates clean. Brush the onion, brinjal, courgettes, tomatoes and red pepper all over with oil and season evenly with salt and pepper. Braai the vegetables over *direct medium heat*, with the lid closed a much as possible, until tender, turning once. The onion will take 10–12 minutes; the brinjal 8–10 minutes, and the courgettes, tomatoes and pepper will take 6–8 minutes. Transfer the vegetables to a cutting board as they are done. When cool enough to handle, chop the vegetables into 1.5-cm pieces.

3. In a medium sauté pan over medium-high heat, warm 1 tablespoon oil. Add the garlic and cook for 1–2 minutes, stirring occasionally. Stir in the braaied vegetables, basil and vinegar, and season with salt and pepper. Serve warm.

SERVES: 4

STUFFED COURGETTES

PREP TIME: 15 minutes
BRAAIING TIME: about 9 minutes
LEVEL OF SPICINESS: 1/10

Stuffing

1 tablespoon extra-virgin olive oil
2 tablespoons finely chopped red onion
¼ teaspoon crushed garlic
½ cup dried breadcrumbs
½ cup grated mozzarella cheese
1 tablespoon finely chopped fresh mint leaves
½ teaspoon coarse sea salt

4–6 large courgettes, ends trimmed,
    each halved lengthways
Extra-virgin olive oil
¼ cup freshly grated Parmesan-style cheese

1. Prepare the braai for direct cooking over medium heat 180°–230°C (350°–450°F).

2. In a medium sauté pan over medium-high heat, warm the oil. Add the onion and cook until tender, 4–5 minutes, stirring occasionally. Add the garlic and cook for 1 minute, stirring occasionally. Add the breadcrumbs and continue to cook until light golden brown, about 2 minutes, stirring occasionally. Transfer to a medium bowl. Add the remaining stuffing ingredients and mix well.

3. Brush the cooking grates clean. Lightly brush the courgettes all over with oil and braai, skin side down first, over *direct medium heat*, with the lid closed as much as possible, about 6 minutes, turning once. Remove from the braai and leave to cool slightly.

4. Using the tip of a teaspoon, scoop out the courgettes' partially cooked flesh to within 0.5 cm of the skin. Finely chop the courgette flesh and add to the stuffing ingredients. Mix well. Carefully spoon the stuffing into the courgette shells, mounding slightly. Scatter the cheese over the top.

5. Braai the stuffed courgettes, skin side down, over *direct medium heat*, with the lid closed, until the stuffing is heated through, about 3 minutes. Serve warm.

SERVES: 4 to 6

Side dishes

SPICY PEPERONATA WITH CAPERS

PREP TIME: 15 minutes
BRAAIING TIME: 12 to 15 minutes
LEVEL OF SPICINESS: 3/10

4 large peppers, preferably 2 red, 1 yellow
    and 1 green
2 tablespoons extra-virgin olive oil
2 garlic cloves, peeled and thinly sliced
1 teaspoon dried origanum
½ teaspoon crushed red chilli flakes
3 tablespoons capers, drained and rinsed
2 tablespoons red wine vinegar
½ teaspoon coarse sea salt
½ teaspoon ground black pepper

1. Prepare the braai for direct cooking over medium heat 180°–230°C (350°–450°F).

2. Brush the cooking grates clean. Braai the peppers over *direct medium heat*, with the lid closed as much as possible, until the skins are blackened and blistered all over, 12–15 minutes, turning occasionally. Place the peppers in a large bowl and cover with cling wrap to trap the steam. Set aside for at least 10 minutes, then remove the peppers from the bowl and discard the charred skins, tops and seeds. Cut the peppers into 1.5-cm strips.

3. In a large heavy-based pan over medium heat, warm the oil. Add the garlic and origanum and cook until the garlic is softened but not browned, about 2 minutes, stirring often. Remove from the heat and stir in the red chilli flakes. Add the pepper strips, capers and vinegar and mix well. Season with the salt and pepper. Transfer to a bowl and leave to cool. Serve at room temperature. If not using right away, cover and refrigerate for up to 3 days.

SERVES: 6

FENNEL, RED PEPPER AND MOZZARELLA SALAD

PREP TIME: 15 minutes
BRAAIING TIME: 20 to 25 minutes
LEVEL OF SPICINESS: 2/10

Dressing

3 tablespoons extra-virgin olive oil
1 tablespoon red wine vinegar
1 teaspoon crushed garlic
¾ teaspoon anchovy paste
¼ teaspoon crushed red chilli flakes
¼ teaspoon coarse sea salt

Salad

2 medium fennel bulbs, stalks and fronds removed,
    with the root ends intact
2 roasted red peppers, cut into 1.5-cm dice
225 grams fresh mozzarella, cut into 1.5-cm dice
½ cup pitted black olives, rinsed and
    roughly chopped
3 tablespoons roughly chopped fresh basil leaves

Coarse sea salt
Ground black pepper

1. Prepare the braai for direct and indirect cooking over medium heat 180°–230°C (350°– 450°F).

2. In a small bowl, whisk the dressing ingredients.

3. Cut each fennel bulb in half through the stem. Lightly brush the bulbs on all sides with some of the dressing.

4. In a large bowl, combine the peppers, mozzarella, olives and basil.

5. Brush the cooking grates clean. Braai the fennel halves, cut side down first, over **direct medium heat**, with the lid closed as much as possible, until lightly charred but not burned, 5–7 minutes. Turn the fennel over and braai for another 3 minutes. Slide the fennel over indirect heat and continue braaiing over **indirect medium heat**, with the lid closed as much as possible, until crisp-tender when pierced with the tip of a knife, 12–15 minutes. Remove from the braai and leave to cool.

6. When the fennel is cool enough to handle, trim away each half's tough, white triangular core. Cut the remaining fennel into 1.5-cm pieces. Add these to the bowl with the salad ingredients. Add as much of the remaining dressing as you like to moisten the salad. Mix well. Season with salt and pepper. Serve at room temperature.

SERVES: 6

Side dishes

COLESLAW WITH JALAPEÑO, CORIANDER AND LIME

PREP TIME: 30 minutes
CHILLING TIME: at least 2 hours
LEVEL OF SPICINESS: 3/10

1 large green cabbage, about 1 kg, thinly sliced
1 medium red pepper, thinly sliced
3 spring onions (white and light green parts only),
    thinly sliced
⅓ cup loosely packed fresh coriander leaves,
    finely chopped
2 medium jalapeño chillies, seeded and finely
    chopped
Grated zest of 1 lime
¼ cup fresh lime juice
2 tablespoons honey
2 teaspoons crushed garlic
Coarse sea salt
Ground black pepper
⅔ cup extra-virgin olive oil

1. In a large bowl, combine the cabbage, red pepper, spring onions, coriander and jalapeños.

2. In a small bowl, whisk the lime zest and juice, honey, garlic, 1 teaspoon salt and ½ teaspoon pepper. Gradually whisk in oil. Pour over the cabbage mixture and mix well. Season with salt and pepper to taste.

3. Cover with cling wrap and refrigerate for at least 2 hours. Stir well to incorporate any juices that may have seeped to the bottom of the bowl. Serve chilled.

SERVES: 8

SPICY CARROT AND DAIKON RADISH SLAW

PREP TIME: 20 minutes
LEVEL OF SPICINESS: 6/10

Slaw

2 cups shredded Chinese cabbage
1 large carrot, cut into matchsticks
1 small daikon radish, cut into matchsticks
2 tablespoons finely chopped fresh mint leaves

Dressing

1 tablespoon peeled, finely grated fresh ginger
1 tablespoon seasoned rice vinegar
1 tablespoon hot chilli-garlic sauce,
    such as Sriracha
1 tablespoon grapeseed oil
2 teaspoons fish sauce
1 teaspoon sugar
1 garlic clove, crushed

1. In a large bowl, combine the slaw ingredients.

2. In a small bowl, whisk the dressing ingredients until thoroughly combined. Pour the dressing over the slaw and toss to coat. Cover and refrigerate until ready to use.

SERVES: 4

CHARRED CORN SALAD

PREP TIME: 15 minutes
BRAAIING TIME: 10 to 15 minutes
LEVEL OF SPICINESS: 2/10

3 fresh sweetcorn mealies, husks removed
Vegetable oil
¼ cup finely diced red pepper
¼ cup finely diced red onion
1 teaspoon finely chopped jalapeño chilli,
    with seeds

Vinaigrette

1 tablespoon Dijon mustard
1 tablespoon white wine vinegar
1 tablespoon sugar
1 tablespoon finely chopped fresh dill
¼ teaspoon coarse sea salt

1. Prepare the braai for direct cooking over medium heat 180°–230°C (350°–450°F).

2. Brush the cooking grates clean. Brush the corn cobs all over with oil. Braai over *direct medium heat*, with the lid closed as much as possible, until browned in spots and tender, 10–15 minutes, turning occasionally. Remove from the braai and, when cool enough to handle, cut the kernels from the cobs (you should have about 2 cups). In a large bowl, combine the sweetcorn, pepper, onion and jalapeño.

4. In a saucepan, whisk the vinaigrette ingredients, including 3 tablespoons oil. Bring to a simmer over medium-high heat, then pour the warm vinaigrette over the corn mixture; toss well. Leave to stand at room temperature until ready to serve.

SERVES: 4

Side dishes

SWEET PEACH CHUTNEY

PREP TIME: 15 minutes, plus about
20 minutes cooking time
LEVEL OF SPICINESS: 2/10

¼ cup packed light brown sugar
2 tablespoons cider vinegar
2 tablespoons peeled, crushed fresh ginger
1 teaspoon mustard powder
1 cinnamon stick
½ teaspoon crushed red chilli flakes
1 medium onion, quartered and thinly sliced
3 ripe peaches, peeled and coarsely chopped

1. In a medium saucepan, combine the brown
sugar, vinegar, ginger, mustard powder, cinnamon
stick and red chilli flakes. Bring to a boil. Add the
onions and simmer over low heat until tender,
about 10 minutes. Add the peaches and simmer over
medium heat until the mixture is slightly thickened,
about 10 minutes, stirring frequently. Remove from
the heat and cool to room temperature. Discard the
cinnamon stick. The chutney can be stored in the
refrigerator, covered, for up to 3 days. Bring to room
temperature before serving.

SERVES: 6 to 8

VIETNAMESE CHOPPED SALAD

PREP TIME: 30 minutes
CHILLING TIME: 10 minutes
LEVEL OF SPICINESS: 7/10

Dressing
¼ cup fish sauce
¼ cup fresh lime juice
¼ cup finely shredded carrot
3 green Thai chillies, thinly sliced
1 tablespoon sugar
1 tablespoon rice vinegar
2 garlic cloves, crushed

Salad
2 tomatoes, seeded and cut into 0.5-cm dice
1 cucumber, peeled, seeded and cut into 0.5-cm dice
1 large daikon radish, peeled and cut into 0.5-cm dice
½ small red onion, cut into 0.5-cm dice
24 fresh basil leaves, coarsely chopped
24 fresh mint leaves, coarsely chopped
⅓ cup fresh coriander leaves
¼ cup dry-roasted unsalted peanuts,
    coarsely chopped

1. In a large serving bowl, whisk the dressing
ingredients until the sugar dissolves.

2. Add the salad ingredients to the bowl with the
dressing, and toss to coat evenly. Refrigerate for
10 minutes to blend the flavours. Serve right away.

SERVES: 6 to 8

ASIAN NOODLE AND VEGETABLE SALAD

PREP TIME: 30 minutes
CHILLING TIME: 2 to 8 hours
LEVEL OF SPICINESS: 2/10

250 grams fresh snow peas, trimmed
2 medium carrots, cut on the diagonal into
    thin slices
300 grams dried Chinese egg noodles, soba noodles
    or spaghetti
1 medium red pepper, cut into 0.5-cm strips
3 large spring onions (white and light green parts
    only), thinly sliced
3 tablespoons finely chopped fresh coriander leaves

Dressing

¼ cup peeled fresh ginger, grated on the
    large holes of a box grater
¼ cup soy sauce
¼ cup rice vinegar
2 tablespoons toasted sesame oil
2 teaspoons honey
2 garlic cloves, crushed
½ teaspoon hot chilli-garlic sauce, such as Sriracha

1 tablespoon toasted sesame seeds

1. Bring a large pot of salted water to a boil. Add the snow peas and cook until they turn bright green, about 30 seconds. Using a fine-mesh strainer, transfer the snow peas to a bowl of iced water. Add the carrots to the boiling water and cook until just crisp-tender, about 2 minutes. Use the strainer to transfer the carrots to the bowl with the snow peas and leave to stand for 2 minutes to cool. Drain the vegetables and pat dry with paper towels.

2. Add the noodles to the boiling water and cook according to package directions. Drain the noodles in a large colander and rinse under cold running water. Transfer the noodles to a large bowl and add the snow peas, carrots, red pepper, spring onions and coriander.

3. Working over a medium bowl, squeeze the grated ginger in your fist to release the juice; discard the ginger solids. You should have about 2 tablespoons of ginger juice. Add the remaining dressing ingredients and whisk well. Pour over the noodle mixture and mix gently with tongs until all the noodles are coated.

4. Cover and refrigerate for at least 2 hours or up to 8 hours. Scatter with the sesame seeds and serve chilled or at room temperature.

SERVES: 6 to 8

Side dishes

RÖSTI WITH BACON AND ONION

PREP TIME: 10 minutes, plus about
1 hour to cook the rösti
CHILLING TIME: 2 to 24 hours
LEVEL OF SPICINESS: 1/10

250 grams potatoes, unpeeled, scrubbed
4 slices streaky bacon, cut into 2.5-cm pieces
3 tablespoons canola oil, as needed
1 tablespoon unsalted butter
1 large onion, finely chopped (about 1½ cups)
Coarse sea salt
Ground black pepper

1. Put the whole potatoes into a large pot, and add enough cold, salted water to cover them by 3 cm. Put a lid on the pot and bring to a boil over high heat. Set the pot lid ajar and reduce the heat to medium-high. Briskly simmer until the potatoes are tender when pierced with a knife, 30–35 minutes. Drain and return the potatoes to the pot. Fill the pot with cold water and leave to stand for 5 minutes to partially cool the potatoes. Drain again, transfer the potatoes to a bowl, and refrigerate for at least 2 hours or up to 24 hours.

2. In a small nonstick pan over medium-high heat, cook the bacon until crisp, 7–8 minutes, stirring occasionally. Using a slotted spoon, transfer the bacon to paper towels to drain. Pour the bacon fat into a small liquid measuring cup and add enough canola oil to measure ¼ cup total. Wipe the pan with paper towels. Melt the butter in the same pan over medium heat. Add the onion and cook until tender and golden, 5–6 minutes, stirring occasionally. Season with ⅛ teaspoon salt and ⅛ teaspoon pepper. Transfer the onion to a bowl. Wipe the pan again with paper towels.

3. Peel the chilled potatoes. Working over a large bowl, shred the potatoes using the large holes of a box grater. Season with 1½ teaspoons salt and ½ teaspoon pepper and mix gently.

4. In the same pan over medium heat, warm 2 tablespoons of the bacon fat mixture. Spread half of the shredded potatoes evenly in the pan. Scatter the bacon and the onions over the potatoes, and then spread the remaining potatoes on top. Using a spatula, lightly pat the potatoes into a cake. Cook until the underside is golden brown, 8–10 minutes.

5. Carefully slide the potato cake out of the pan onto a plate. Place a second plate over the potato cake and invert it, so the browned side is facing up. Warm the remaining bacon fat mixture in the pan over medium heat. Gently slide the potato cake, browned side up, back into the pan. Cook until the second side is browned, 8–10 minutes. Slide the potato cake onto a serving plate, gently pressing it back together, if necessary, if some pieces break off. Cut into wedges, and serve hot.

SERVES: 6

SMOKY NEW POTATOES WITH SPICY AÏOLI

PREP TIME: 10 minutes
BRAAIING TIME: 15 to 20 minutes
SPECIAL EQUIPMENT: perforated grill pan
or large cast-iron pan
LEVEL OF SPICINESS: 7/10

Aïoli

½ cup mayonnaise
1 tablespoon extra-virgin olive oil
2 teaspoons fresh lemon juice
1 teaspoon Tabasco sauce
1 teaspoon crushed garlic
½ teaspoon saffron threads, crumbled (optional)

2 teaspoons smoked paprika
1 teaspoon coarse sea salt
½ teaspoon ground cayenne pepper
½ teaspoon ground black pepper
1 kg small new potatoes, halved
2 tablespoons extra-virgin olive oil
2 teaspoons crushed garlic
2 tablespoons roughly chopped fresh Italian
    parsley leaves

1. In a small bowl, whisk the aïoli ingredients.

2. In a large bowl, combine the paprika, salt, cayenne pepper and black pepper. Add the potatoes, oil and garlic. Toss to coat the potatoes evenly.

3. Prepare the braai for direct cooking over medium heat 180°–230°C (350°–450°F) and place a perforated grill pan on the braai to preheat.

4. Spread the potatoes in a single layer on the grill pan and braai over **direct medium heat**, with the lid closed as much as possible, until lightly browned and tender, 15–20 minutes, turning occasionally. Transfer to a serving bowl.

5. Sprinkle the chopped parsley over the potatoes. Serve with the aïoli.

SERVES: 4 to 6

Side dishes

SPICY MAPLE BAKED BEANS

PREP TIME: 15 minutes, plus about
1 hour for the beans
LEVEL OF SPICINESS: 5/10

1 tablespoon vegetable oil
1 medium onion, finely chopped
360 grams gammon steak, trimmed and finely diced
1 tablespoon crushed garlic
3 cans (400 grams each) baked beans
¾ cup maple syrup
2 tablespoons tomato paste
1 tablespoon Worcestershire sauce
1 tablespoon prepared chilli powder
¼ teaspoon ground cayenne pepper
1 tablespoon prepared English mustard
Coarse sea salt
Ground black pepper

1. In a large saucepan over medium-low heat, warm
the oil. Cook the onion until soft, 8–10 minutes,
stirring occasionally. Add the gammon and the garlic
and cook for 2 minutes more, stirring occasionally.
Add the baked beans, maple syrup, tomato paste,
Worcestershire sauce, chilli powder and cayenne
pepper. Bring to a boil over high heat. Lower the heat
to medium and continue cooking, uncovered, for
about 45 minutes, stirring once or twice.

2. Just before serving, add the mustard and season
with salt and pepper. Serve warm.

SERVES: 8

RAISIN-PINE NUT COUSCOUS

PREP TIME: 20 minutes
LEVEL OF SPICINESS: 1/10

½ cup pine nuts or raw almonds
1 cup fresh orange juice
½ cup water
⅓ cup raisins or sultanas
2 tablespoons unsalted butter
1 tablespoon fresh lime juice
1 teaspoon peeled, grated fresh ginger
1 teaspoon coarse sea salt
½ teaspoon ground black pepper
1 cup quick-cooking couscous
⅓ cup finely chopped fresh mint leaves

1. In a small sauté pan over medium heat, toast the
pine nuts until golden brown, about 5 minutes,
stirring occasionally. Set aside.

2. In a medium saucepan, combine the orange juice,
water, raisins, butter, lime juice, ginger, salt and
black pepper. Bring to a boil over high heat.
Stir in the couscous, cover, and remove from the
heat. Allow the couscous to absorb the liquid for
5–10 minutes. Fluff the couscous with a fork and
transfer to a serving dish. Add the toasted pine nuts
and the chopped mint. Stir gently. Serve warm or
at room temperature.

SERVES: 4

BROWN RICE SALAD WITH LIME DRESSING

PREP TIME: 15 minutes
LEVEL OF SPICINESS: 1/10

1½ cups brown rice

Dressing
¼ cup vegetable oil
2 tablespoons rice vinegar
2 tablespoons fresh lime juice
1 teaspoon toasted sesame oil
1 teaspoon crushed garlic
½ teaspoon coarse sea salt
¼ teaspoon ground black pepper

1 large carrot, peeled and grated or finely chopped
½ cup chopped unsalted, dry-roasted peanuts
3 spring onions, root ends trimmed, cut across into
    thin slices
3 tablespoons finely chopped fresh coriander leaves

1. Cook the rice according to package directions. Drain, rinse under cold water, and shake off the excess moisture.

2. In a large bowl, whisk the dressing ingredients.

3. Add the cooked rice, carrot, peanuts, spring onions and coriander to the bowl with the dressing. Toss to blend. Serve warm or at room temperature.

SERVES: 4 to 6

Seasonings

Don't let your food be bland and forgettable. At the very least, season it with a lively blend of herbs and spices before it goes onto the braai. The blends offered here are ordered from fairly mild to seriously hot, so pick your preferred level of firepower and see how it feels. Each mixture features some degree of capsaicin, meaning you will definitely feel something on your tongue – not just a taste like saltiness or sweetness; but a sensation that tickles the nerve endings and sometimes lingers long after the flavours have faded.

If you would rather not make your own spice blend, most supermarkets carry a good selection. Almost every culture in the world has contributed some clever combination of herbs and spices. Classic examples include Indian curry powder (a blend of ground spices), herbes de Provence (a mix of dried herbs with a French accent), and jerk seasoning (a potent combination featuring chillies, allspice, peppercorns, cinnamon and salt).

Salt really should be part of any seasoning. If it is not in a store-bought blend, add it. Salt amplifies the other flavours and satisfies a basic human craving. Coarse sea salt or flaked salt are particularly good for braaiing, because they have a pure, clean taste and adhere to the surface of food, staying there rather than falling off. But I can't mention salt without pepper, as each complements the other.

Peppercorns originated from a bush that grows wild in the tropics. In southwest India, famous for the spectacular Tellicherry peppercorns, the bushes are trained on tall trellises and the berries mature slowly on the vine until they turn greenish yellow. They are then harvested and dried in the sun until their skins harden and darken to black. Most often we grind peppercorns and use the powder (either fine or coarse) right away, but to get the maximum effect of peppercorns and other dried spices, like cumin seed, toast them in a dry pan over medium heat for a few minutes. The heat will volatilize the oils inside the spices, giving the flavours and aromas a big push. Just remember to shake the pan often to avoid scorching the spices and turning them bitter.

Toasted Cumin and Origanum

GOOD ON: pork, chicken and seafood
MAKES: about 3 tablespoons
SPECIAL EQUIPMENT: spice mill
LEVEL OF SPICINESS: 4/10

1 tablespoon cumin seed
2 teaspoons dried origanum
2 teaspoons packed light brown sugar
2 teaspoons coarse sea salt
½ teaspoon prepared chilli powder
¼ teaspoon ground black pepper

1. In a small pan over medium heat, toast the cumin seed until fragrant, 2–3 minutes, shaking the pan occasionally to prevent burning. Pour into a spice mill and leave to cool. Grind the cumin seed into a powder and combine with the remaining ingredients.

Toasted Sesame Salt
GOOD ON: chicken, seafood and vegetables
MAKES: about 2 tablespoons
LEVEL OF SPICINESS: 5/10

1 tablespoon white sesame seeds
2 teaspoons coarse sea salt
1 teaspoon garlic flakes
1 teaspoon ground black pepper

1. In a pan over medium heat, toast the sesame seeds until barely golden brown, 2–3 minutes, shaking the pan to prevent burning. Pour into a bowl and leave to cool. Add the remaining ingredients and mix well.

Red Alert
GOOD ON: pork, chicken and seafood
MAKES: 2½ tablespoons
LEVEL OF SPICINESS: 7/10

1 tablespoon smoked paprika
2 teaspoons coarse sea salt
1 teaspoon ground black pepper
½ teaspoon onion flakes
½ teaspoon dried thyme
½ teaspoon ground cayenne pepper

1. In a small bowl, mix the ingredients.

Pepper Power
GOOD ON: red meat and pork
MAKES: about ¼ cup
SPECIAL EQUIPMENT: spice mill
LEVEL OF SPICINESS: 8/10

1 tablespoon black peppercorns
1 tablespoon white peppercorns
1 teaspoon crushed red chilli flakes
1 tablespoon coarse sea salt
1 teaspoon ground cumin
½ teaspoon ground coriander

1. In a small pan over medium heat, toast the black and white peppercorns until fragrant, 2–3 minutes, shaking the pan occasionally to prevent burning. Pour into a spice mill and leave to cool. Add the crushed red chilli flakes to the peppercorns and grind into a powder. Pour the powder into a small bowl and mix well with the remaining ingredients.

Chilli Madness
GOOD ON: red meat and pork
MAKES: 2½ tablespoons
LEVEL OF SPICINESS: 9/10

2 teaspoons coarse sea salt
2 teaspoons packed light brown sugar
1 teaspoon prepared chilli powder
1 teaspoon ancho chilli powder
1 teaspoon chipotle chilli powder
½ teaspoon ground cayenne pepper

1. In a small bowl, mix the ingredients.

Sauces

Say what you will about a food like a chicken breast. Maybe it was braaied to perfection and it drips with succulent juices, but chicken is just chicken until you taste it against the backdrop of other flavours. When you add an interesting sauce, chicken or any other main ingredient reveals itself as either very different or very similar to the sauce. Suddenly, the main ingredient is dressed with a certain style and we taste more character in the dish. That's the point of the following sauces: more hot and spicy character for whatever you happen to be braaiing.

Blazing Hot Habanero-Rum Sauce

MAKES: about ¼ cup
BRAAIING TIME: about 6 minutes
SPECIAL EQUIPMENT: perforated grill pan, rubber gloves
LEVEL OF SPICINESS: 10/10

12 habanero chillies, about 60 grams total
12 large garlic cloves, peeled
3 tablespoons white rum
Finely grated zest of 1 lime
3 tablespoons fresh lime juice
1 teaspoon coarse sea salt

1. Prepare the braai for direct cooking over medium heat 180°–230°C (350°–450°F) and place a perforated grill pan on the braai to preheat.

2. Wearing rubber gloves (to avoid burning your skin), remove and discard the stems and seeds from the habaneros. Cut each habanero in half. Spread the garlic cloves and the habaneros in a single layer on the grill pan and braai over *direct medium heat,* with the lid closed as much as possible, until the garlic cloves are golden brown and the habaneros are blistered, about 6 minutes, turning occasionally. Remove from the braai.

3. In a blender with a glass container (the sauce could stain a plastic container), process the garlic and the habaneros until finely chopped. Add the remaining ingredients and purée (avoid inhaling the vapours while blending). Strain through a fine-mesh strainer into a small glass bowl and discard the solids. Transfer the sauce to a bowl, cover and leave to stand for at least 1 hour to blend the flavours. Serve at room temperature. If not using right away, cover and refrigerate for up to 2 weeks.

Spring Onion, Ginger and Green Chilli Sauce

MAKES: about 1 cup
LEVEL OF SPICINESS: 5/10

8 large spring onions (white and light green
    parts only), finely chopped
¼ cup peeled, crushed fresh ginger
4 teaspoons soy sauce
4 teaspoons rice vinegar
1 tablespoon toasted sesame oil
2 garlic cloves, crushed
1 small Thai green chilli, with seeds, finely chopped

1. In a small bowl, mash and mix the ingredients.
Serve immediately. (The sauce can be covered and
refrigerated for up to 2 days.)

Hot Pepper Steak Sauce

MAKES: about ½ cup
LEVEL OF SPICINESS: 5/10

¼ cup (60 grams) unsalted butter, melted
2 tablespoons Worcestershire sauce
1 tablespoon Chinese-style chilli-garlic paste
1 tablespoon spicy brown (French) mustard
1 tablespoon hot chilli-garlic sauce,
    such as Sriracha
½ teaspoon ground black pepper
¼ teaspoon coarse sea salt

1. In a small bowl, whisk all the ingredients until
smooth. If not using right away, cover and refrigerate
for up to 2 months (when cold, the sauce may
become semi-solid; if so, warm gently to liquefy).

NOTE!
This spicy version of a traditional tangy brown
British steak sauce is less sweet than popular
commercial brands. It is a quick and clever way
to dress up braaied meats and an impressive
tool for bolstering your do-it-yourself credibility
at the table.

Sauces

Portuguese Piri-Piri Hot Sauce
MAKES: about ⅔ cup
LEVEL OF SPICINESS: 10/10

12 small red or green (Bird's-eye) chillies, with
    seeds, coarsely chopped
3 garlic cloves, crushed and peeled
2 tablespoons sherry vinegar or red wine vinegar
Finely grated zest of 1 lemon
½ teaspoon coarse sea salt
½ cup extra-virgin olive oil

1. In a blender with a glass container (the sauce
could stain a plastic container), combine the chillies,
garlic, vinegar, lemon zest and salt and blend until
the chillies are very finely chopped. With the motor
running, slowly add the oil in a thin stream until the
mixture is thoroughly combined (avoid inhaling the
vapours while blending). Transfer to a bowl, cover,
and leave to stand for at least 1 hour to blend the
flavours. Serve at room temperature. (The sauce
can be covered and refrigerated for up to 1 month.)

Charred Jalapeño Stilton Butter
MAKES: about ½ cup
LEVEL OF SPICINESS: 3/10

3 large jalapeño chillies
100 grams Stilton cheese, without rind, crumbled
2 tablespoons unsalted butter, softened
2 tablespoons extra-virgin olive oil
1 small garlic clove, crushed
Coarse sea salt
Ground black pepper

1. Put the jalapeños over a gas burner set to
medium heat or under a grill and char the skins all
over, 4–6 minutes, turning as needed. Transfer to
a cutting board and, when cool enough to handle,
finely chop them, discarding the seeds and ribs
for a milder flavour. Combine with the remaining
ingredients, including salt and pepper to taste.

2. If not using the butter right away, store in a tightly
sealed container and refrigerate for up to 1 week.
Bring to room temperature before serving.

Spicy Curry Sauce with Coconut Milk

MAKES: about 3 cups
LEVEL OF SPICINESS: 5/10

1 tablespoon canola oil
1 medium onion, finely chopped (about 1½ cups)
2 tablespoons peeled, crushed fresh ginger
2 garlic cloves, crushed
1 small Thai chilli, with seeds, finely chopped
1 tablespoon curry powder
1 can (400 ml) coconut milk, shaken
1¼ teaspoons finely grated lime zest
3 tablespoons fresh lime juice
1 tablespoon soy sauce
1 tablespoon tomato paste
½ teaspoon coarse sea salt

1. In a medium saucepan over medium heat, warm the oil. Add the onion, ginger, garlic and chilli and cook until the onion is golden, about 5 minutes, stirring occasionally. Add the curry powder and stir until fragrant, about 30 seconds. Add the coconut milk, lime zest, lime juice, soy sauce and tomato paste and bring to a boil, whisking well to dissolve the tomato paste. Reduce the heat to medium-low and simmer until the sauce is lightly thickened, about 5 minutes, stirring occasionally. Season with the salt. Serve warm. (The sauce can be cooled, then covered and refrigerated for up to 2 days. If it thickens, thin with water by the tablespoonful, as needed.)

Siren Steak Sauce

MAKES: about ⅔ cup
LEVEL OF SPICINESS: 4/10

½ cup dry red wine
½ cup tomato purée
½ cup water
¼ cup dark molasses
2 tablespoons red wine vinegar
1 tablespoon Dijon mustard
1 tablespoon Worcestershire sauce
½ teaspoon chilli powder
½ teaspoon celery seed
½ teaspoon coarse sea salt
¼ teaspoon curry powder
¼ teaspoon ground cumin

1. In a medium saucepan, combine all the ingredients and mix well. Bring to a simmer over medium heat and cook, uncovered, until about ⅔ cup remains, about 30 minutes, stirring occasionally. Remove from the heat and cool to room temperature.

Index

Index

Index

Index

Safety guidelines

Please read your Owner's Guide and familiarize yourself with and follow all 'dangers', 'warnings' and 'cautions'. Also follow the braaiing procedures and maintenance requirements listed in your Owner's Guide. If you cannot locate the Owner's Guide for your grill model, please contact the manufacturer prior to use. If you have any questions concerning the 'dangers', 'warnings' and 'cautions' contained in your Weber® gas, electric or charcoal grill Owner's Guide, or if you do not have an Owner's Guide for your specific model, please visit **www.weber.com** to access your Owner's Guide before using your grill.